gets you through

EDEXCEL A-LEVEL
MATHS
PRACTICE TEST PAPERS

ANOUK DE VOS

Contents

ACKNOWLEDGEMENTS

The author and publisher are grateful to the copyright holders for permission to use quoted materials and images.

Cover and page 1: © Shutterstock.com/Napat

Every effort has been made to trace copyright holders and obtain their permission for the use of copyright material. The author and publisher will gladly receive information enabling them to rectify any error or omission in subsequent editions. All facts are correct at time of going to press.

Published by Letts Educational
An imprint of HarperCollins*Publishers*
1 London Bridge Street
London SE1 9GF
ISBN: 9780008276218

First published 2018

10 9 8 7 6 5 4 3 2 1

© HarperCollins*Publishers* Limited 2018

British Library Cataloguing in Publication Data.

A CIP record of this book is available from the British Library.

Commissioning Editor: Gillian Bowman
Author: Anouk de Vos
Project Management: Mark Steward
Review and Copyediting: Rachel and Nick Hamar
Answer Checking: Paul Winters
Cover Design: Paul Oates
Inside Concept Design: Ian Wrigley
Text Design and Layout: Jouve India
Production: Natalia Rebow
Printed in the UK

Name: ....

Mathematics

Advanced Paper 1: Pure Mathematics 1 Time allowed: 2 hours

You must have:

Calculator

Mathematical Formulae (see pages 84–7)

Statistical Tables

Statistical tables are available on the Edexcel website. They can also be found on a calculator.

Candidates may use any calculator allowed by the regulations of the Joint Council for Qualifications. Calculators must not have the facility for symbolic algebra manipulation, differentiation and integration, or have retrievable mathematical formulae stored in them.

Instructions

- Use **black** ink or ball-point pen.
- If pencil is used for diagrams/sketches/graphs it must be dark (HB or B). Coloured pencils and highlighter pens must not be used.
- **Fill in the box** on the top of the page with your name.
- Answer **all** questions and ensure that your answers to parts of questions are clearly labelled.
- Answer the questions in the space provided after each question.
  - *if you require extra space please use a blank piece of paper.*
- You should show sufficient working to make your methods clear. Answers without working may not gain full credit.
- When a calculator is used, the answer should be given to an appropriate degree of accuracy.

Information

- The total mark for this paper is 100.
- The marks for **each** question are shown in brackets
  - *use this as a guide as to how much time to spend on each question.*

Advice

- Read each question carefully before you start to answer it.
- Try to answer every question.
- Check your answers if you have time at the end.

1. A geometric series begins

$$30 + 18 + 10.8 + 6.48 + \ldots$$

Find the common ratio of the series.

....

....

....

....

(Total 2 marks)

2. Find the equation of the line that is perpendicular to $y = 5x - 3$ and passes through the point $(2, 7)$

....

....

....

(Total 2 marks)

3. (a) Find the value of n for which $\sqrt{27} = 3^n$ **(2)**

....

....

....

....

(b) Hence solve the equation $3^{2x} = \sqrt{27}$ **(1)**

....

....

....

(Total 3 marks)

4. Describe the geometrical transformation that maps the curve with equation $y = \sin x$ onto the curves with equations:

(a) $y = 3\sin x$ **(2)**

(b) $y = \sin(x + 45°)$ **(2)**

(c) $y = -\sin x$ **(2)**

(Total 6 marks)

5. Prove by exhaustion that $n^2 + 1$ is not divisible by 3, for $8 \leqslant n \leqslant 12$, given that n is an integer.

(Total 4 marks)

6. Given that $x = \dfrac{1}{\cos\theta}$, use the quotient rule to show that $\dfrac{\mathrm{d}x}{\mathrm{d}\theta} = \tan\theta\sec\theta$

(Total 3 marks)

7. Using the binomial expansion, express $(1 + x)^3$ in ascending powers of x, up to x^3

(Total 3 marks)

8. Giving your answers as simply as possible, find $\dfrac{dy}{dx}$ when:

(a) $y = (4x + 1)^3$ **(2)**

(b) $y = \ln(4x + 1)$ **(2)**

(c) $y = (4x + 1)^3 \ln(4x + 1)$ **(3)**

(Total 7 marks)

9. (a) Express $\dfrac{5 + \sqrt{3}}{3 + \sqrt{3}}$ in the form $\dfrac{m - \sqrt{3}}{n}$, where m and n are integers. **(4)**

(b) Express $\sqrt{32} + \dfrac{10}{\sqrt{2}}$ in the form $k\sqrt{2}$ **(3)**

(Total 7 marks)

10. The functions f and g are defined by

$$f(x) = \sqrt{2x + 4}, \text{ for real values of } x, x \geqslant -2$$

$$g(x) = \frac{1}{2x + 1}, \text{ for real values of } x, \ x \neq -\frac{1}{2}$$

(a) Find the range of f **(2)**

....

....

....

(b) The inverse of f is f⁻¹

    (i) Determine $f^{-1}(x)$ **(3)**

....

....

....

....

....

    (ii) Write down the domain of $f^{-1}(x)$ **(1)**

....

....

(c) The composite function fg is denoted by h.

    (i) Find an expression for $h(x)$ **(2)**

....

....

    (ii) Solve the equation $h(x) = 4$ **(3)**

....

....

....

....

(Total 11 marks)

11. A triangular flowerbed has two sides of lengths 10 m and 11 m, as illustrated in the diagram.

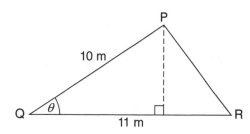

The acute angle of PQR is θ, where $\sin\theta = \dfrac{4}{5}$

(a) Work out the area of the flowerbed. **(2)**

(b) Find the exact value of $\cos\theta$, giving your answer in its simplest form. **(1)**

(c) Calculate the length of the missing side, PR, of the flowerbed.

Give your answer correct to 3 significant figures. **(3)**

(Total 6 marks)

12. The value V of a car t years after January 1st, 2011 is given by

$$V = 15000 \times (1.2)^{-t}$$

(a) Determine the value of the car on January 1st, 2015. **(2)**

....

....

(b) Calculate t when the value of the car drops below £4000. **(4)**

....

....

....

....

(c) Explain, in context, your solution to part (b). **(1)**

....

(Total 7 marks)

13. The lines l_1 and l_2 have equations

$$r = \begin{bmatrix} -2 \\ 10 \\ 4 \end{bmatrix} + \lambda \begin{bmatrix} -1 \\ 3 \\ 2 \end{bmatrix} \text{ and } r = \begin{bmatrix} 0 \\ 8 \\ 1 \end{bmatrix} + \mu \begin{bmatrix} -1 \\ -1 \\ 1 \end{bmatrix}, \text{ respectively.}$$

(a) Show that l_1 and l_2 intersect and find the coordinates of the point of intersection, P. **(5)**

....

....

....

....

....

....

....

....

(b) Verify that the point Q, given by (–3, 5, 4) lies on l_2 **(2)**

(Total 7 marks)

14. The polynomial p(x) is given by p(x) = $3x^3 + 2x^2 - 19x + k$

(a) Given that $(x - 2)$ is a factor of p(x), show that $k = 6$ **(2)**

(b) Express p(x) as a product of three linear factors. **(3)**

(Total 5 marks)

15. (a) Given that $\dfrac{3}{x^2 - x - 2}$ can be written in the form $\dfrac{A}{x+1} + \dfrac{B}{x-2}$, where A and B are integers, find the values of A and B. Give your answer as partial fractions.

(4)

(b) Hence or otherwise, find $\displaystyle\int \dfrac{3}{x^2 - x - 2}\, \mathrm{d}x$

(3)

(Total 7 marks)

16. Using a suitable substitution, find the exact value of

$$\int_0^1 x\sqrt{2x+1}\ \mathrm{d}x$$

(Total 7 marks)

17. A circle with centre C has equation $(x-8)^2 + (y-15)^2 = 289$

   (a) Give

      (i)   the coordinates of C,   **(1)**

      (ii) the radius of the circle.   **(1)**

   (b) (i) Verify that the circle passes through the origin O   **(1)**

      (ii) The circle passes through the points $(16, 0)$ and $(0, p)$

           Use this information to sketch the circle and find the value of p **(2)**

(Total 5 marks)

18. (a) Sketch the graph of $y = \tan\theta$ for $0° \leqslant \theta \leqslant 360°$ **(1)**

(b) Write down the two solutions of the equation

$\tan\theta = 1.327$, in the interval $0° \leqslant \theta \leqslant 360°$ **(2)**

(c) (i) Given that $\sin\theta + \cos\theta = 0$, show that $\tan\theta = -1$ **(1)**

(ii) Hence solve the equation

$\sin(\theta - 10°) + \cos(\theta - 10°) = 0$, in the interval $0° \leqslant \theta \leqslant 360°$ **(4)**

(Total 8 marks)

Name: _____

Mathematics

Advanced Paper 2: Pure Mathematics 2   Time allowed: 2 hours

You must have:

Calculator

Mathematical Formulae (see pages 84–7)

Statistical Tables

Statistical tables are available on the Edexcel website. They can also be found on a calculator.

Candidates may use any calculator allowed by the regulations of the Joint Council for Qualifications. Calculators must not have the facility for symbolic algebra manipulation, differentiation and integration, or have retrievable mathematical formulae stored in them.

Instructions

- Use **black** ink or ball-point pen.
- If pencil is used for diagrams/sketches/graphs it must be dark (HB or B). Coloured pencils and highlighter pens must not be used.
- **Fill in the box** on the top of the page with your name.
- Answer **all** questions and ensure that your answers to parts of questions are clearly labelled.
- Answer the questions in the space provided after each question.
  - *if you require extra space please use a blank piece of paper.*
- You should show sufficient working to make your methods clear. Answers without working may not gain full credit.
- When a calculator is used, the answer should be given to an appropriate degree of accuracy.

Information

- The total mark for this paper is 100.
- The marks for **each** question are shown in brackets
  - *use this as a guide as to how much time to spend on each question.*

Advice

- Read each question carefully before you start to answer it.
- Try to answer every question.
- Check your answers if you have time at the end.

1. Solve the inequality $x^2 - 6x + 5 \geqslant 0$

....

....

....

(Total 2 marks)

2. Solve $x - 7 = \dfrac{4}{x}$, leaving your answers in surd form.

....

....

....

....

....

....

(Total 3 marks)

3. Use the trapezium rule with 5 strips to find an approximate value for

$$\int_0^1 x^2 e^x \, dx$$

Give your answer correct to 3 significant figures.

....

....

....

....

....

....

....

....

....

(Total 4 marks)

4. A curve is defined by the parametric equations

$$x = \frac{1}{1+t}, y = t^2 + 4$$

(a) Find the corresponding Cartesian equation for the curve. **(2)**

(b) Find the gradient of the curve at the point where $t = 3$ **(4)**

(Total 6 marks)

5. Prove that $\cot^4\theta + \cot^2\theta \equiv \operatorname{cosec}^4\theta - \operatorname{cosec}^2\theta$

(Total 3 marks)

6. (a) Use integration by parts to find the indefinite integral

$$\int x \ln x \, dx$$ **(5)**

(b) Use your answer to part (a) to find the area under the graph of $x \ln x$ between the origin and $x = 4$

Leave your answer in the form $a \ln b + c$, where a, b and c are integers. **(3)**

(Total 8 marks)

7. Use differentiation from first principles to prove that the derivative of $f(x) = 5x^3 - 8x + 4$ is $f^{-1}(x) = 15x^2 - 8$

(Total 6 marks)

8. Prove by contradiction that if x^2 is even, then x must also be even.

(Total 5 marks)

9. (a) Find the general solution to the differential equation $\frac{dy}{dx} = 3x^2(y+1)$

giving y in terms of x (5)

(b) Find the particular solution, given that $y = 5$ when $x = 0$ (2)

(Total 7 marks)

10. Points A and B have position vectors $\mathbf{a} = 9\mathbf{i} - 2\mathbf{j} - 6\mathbf{k}$ and $\mathbf{b} = 2\mathbf{i} - 6\mathbf{j} + 3\mathbf{k}$, respectively.

(a) Find:

    (i) $|\mathbf{a}|$ **(1)**

    (ii) $|\mathbf{b}|$ **(1)**

    (iii) $|\overrightarrow{\mathbf{AB}}|$ **(2)**

(b) Find the angle between $\mathbf{a}$ and $\mathbf{b}$, giving your answer to the nearest degree.   **(3)**

(Total 7 marks)

11. An arithmetic progression has first term 9 and common difference 7.

Find its 12th term, u_{12}

(Total 2 marks)

12. Find $\int \dfrac{3x}{3x^2 + 1}\,\mathrm{d}x$

(Total 4 marks)

13. Solve:

(a) $e^x = 7$ **(1)**

(b) $3^x = 20$ **(2)**

(Total 3 marks)

14. A curve is defined implicitly by $x^2 + y^3 - 4xy = -14$

(a) Find $\dfrac{dy}{dx}$ for this curve.

(6)

(b) Determine the gradient of the curve $x^2 + y^3 - 4xy = -14$ at the point $(1, 2)$

(1)

(Total 7 marks)

15. Solve the following pair of simultaneous equations:

$$2y - 2x + 1 = 0 \qquad \text{and} \qquad x^2 - xy + 2y^2 = 8$$

(Total 7 marks)

16. Use the addition formulae to find the exact value of cos 75°

(Total 5 marks)

17. Find the exact area bounded by the graph of $y = e^{2x}$, the axes and the line $x = 4$

(Total 4 marks)

18. Prove the identity $\tan\theta + \cot\theta \equiv 2\operatorname{cosec}2\theta$

(Total 6 marks)

19. A water tank initially has a depth of 0.5 m and it is filled in such a way that t minutes after the tap is turned on, the increase in depth x is described by the differential equation:

$$\frac{dx}{dt} = \frac{1}{12x\sqrt{3x - 0.5}}$$

Solve the differential equation to find the time t as a function of the depth x

(Total 11 marks)

Mathematics

Advanced Paper 3: Statistics and
Mechanics

Time allowed: 2 hours

You must have:

Calculator

Mathematical Formulae (see pages 84–7)

Statistical Tables

Statistical tables are available on the Edexcel website. They can also be found on
a calculator.

**Candidates may use any calculator allowed by the regulations of the Joint Council for
Qualifications. Calculators must not have the facility for symbolic algebra manipulation,
differentiation and integration, or have retrievable mathematical formulae stored in them.**

Instructions

- Use **black** ink or ball-point pen.
- If pencil is used for diagrams/sketches/graphs it must be dark (HB or B). Coloured pencils and
  highlighter pens must not be used.
- **Fill in the box** on the top of the page with your name.
- Answer **all** questions and ensure that your answers to parts of questions are clearly labelled.
- Answer the questions in the space provided after each question.
  - *if you require extra space please use a blank piece of paper.*
- You should show sufficient working to make your methods clear. Answers without working may
  not gain full credit.
- When a calculator is used, the answer should be given to an appropriate degree of accuracy.

Information

- The total mark for this paper is 100.
- The marks for **each** question are shown in brackets
  - *use this as a guide as to how much time to spend on each question.*

Advice

- Read each question carefully before you start to answer it.
- Try to answer every question.
- Check your answers if you have time at the end.

SECTION A : STATISTICS

1. In a report on catering facilities in the workplace, a survey was conducted in three offices, A, B and C, which employ 140, 176 and 122 people respectively.

   A stratified sample of 40 workers is obtained.

   (a) Work out the percentage of employees selected who are from office A. **(2)**

   ....

   ....

   (b) Calculate the number of employees selected from office C. **(1)**

   ....

   ....

   (Total 3 marks)

2. Below is some information taken from the Large Data Set.

   Figure 1 - Heathrow – daily maximum gust October, 1987 and 2015

   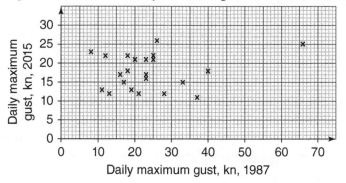

   Figure 2 - Heathrow – daily mean windspeed/maximum gust October 1987

   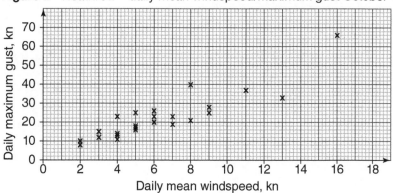

Question 2 continued

(a) Comment on each of each of the scatter diagrams, using your knowledge of the Large
Data Set to account for any outliers where appropriate. **(4)**

(b) John models rainfall for the month of October 2015, in mm per day, using N $(6.47, 1.8^2)$

Use John's model to predict the number of days (to the nearest day) that rainfall is expected
to be below the mean by more than one standard deviation in October. **(2)**

(Total 6 marks)

3. Maria wants to use the Large Data Set to investigate if there is evidence of global warming.

She collects the following data for the mean daily temperature for the last week of June and first week of July (14 days) for both 1987 and 2015, measured in degrees Celsius.

	1987		2015	
Hurn	$\sum x = 238.90$	$\dfrac{\sum(x - \bar{x})^2}{n} = 4.5398$	$\sum x = 243.45$	$\dfrac{\sum(x - \bar{x})^2}{n} = 6.3020$
Beijing	$\sum x = 339.29$	$\dfrac{\sum(x - \bar{x})^2}{n} = 2.1405$	$\sum x = 349.34$	$\dfrac{\sum(x - \bar{x})^2}{n} = 4.0863$
Camborne	$\sum x = 211.65$	$\dfrac{\sum(x - \bar{x})^2}{n} = 1.9518$	$\sum x = 230.10$	$\dfrac{\sum(x - \bar{x})^2}{n} = 1.6840$

(a) Calculate the mean for each location in each year. **(2)**

(b) Calculate the standard deviation for each location and for each year. **(2)**

(c) Do your calculations suggest there is evidence of global warming? Use your knowledge of the Large Data Set where appropriate. Explain your answer. **(3)**

(d) Give two criticisms of Maria's data collection method. **(2)**

(Total 9 marks)

4. Two tetrahedral dice have their faces numbered 1, 2, 3 and 4.

X is the random variable "the sum of the scores when two dice are thrown". The probability distribution for X is given by:

$$P(X = x) = \begin{cases} \dfrac{x-1}{16}, & x = 2,3,4,5 \\ \dfrac{9-x}{16}, & x = 6,7,8 \end{cases}$$

(a) Find the probability that $X = 7$ **(2)**

(b) Find the probability that $X \leqslant 6$ **(4)**

(Total 6 marks)

5. A mathematical puzzle is devised and after running several trials, it is found that the length of time in seconds taken by Year 6 children to solve the puzzle is normally distributed with a mean of 26.4 seconds and a standard deviation of 6.9 seconds.

A Year 6 teacher records the time it takes for 14 pupils in her class to solve the puzzle, as follows:

31.4, 24.1, 43.6, 34.5, 27.8, 19.7, 28.2, 31.1, 33.7, 49.2, 18.6, 24.5, 36.4, 30.3

Investigate, using the 5% significance level, the hypothesis that the mean time taken to solve the puzzle is 26.4 seconds.

(Total 8 marks)

6. The length of time, X, that patients wait in a dentist's waiting room is known to be normally distributed with mean 19 minutes and standard deviation 6 minutes.

(a) Find the probability that Jenny will have to wait more than 25 minutes to see the dentist. **(3)**

(b) What proportion of patients wait less than 12 minutes? **(3)**

(c) Find $P(16 < X < 22)$ **(2)**

(Total 8 marks)

7. Students in Mr Cass's tutor group have dogs, cats or rabbits as pets.

The probability that a student owns a dog, a cat or a rabbit is 0.3, 0.4 and 0.2 respectively.

Calculate the probability that a student chosen randomly from the tutor group:

(a) has a dog, a cat and a rabbit, **(1)**

(b) has no pets, **(1)**

(c) has only a rabbit. **(2)**

(d) The probabilities of having a dog, a cat or a rabbit are independent of each other.

Calculate the probability that a student has exactly one of either a dog, a cat or a rabbit. **(3)**

The probability of Elliot getting a dog is 0.3.

The probability that Alfie gets a dog, given that Elliot also gets a dog, is 0.8.

(e) Calculate the probability that both Alfie and Elliot get a dog. **(3)**

(Total 10 marks)

10. A Formula One car moves from rest on a straight horizontal racetrack. Its motion is modelled by the following graph.

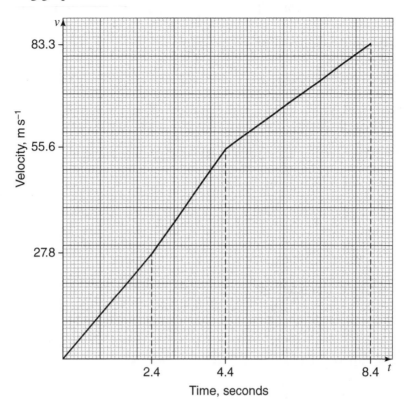

(a) Find the total distance travelled in the first 8.4 seconds of motion. **(4)**

(b) Find the average speed of the car during this time. **(2)**

(Total 6 marks)

11. Three forces act on a particle as follows:

$$F_1: (6\mathbf{i} + 7\mathbf{j}) \qquad F_2: (8\mathbf{i} - 5\mathbf{j}) \qquad F_3: (-4\mathbf{i} + 3\mathbf{j})$$

where **i** and **j** are perpendicular vectors.

(a) Find the resultant of the vectors. **(2)**

(b) Find the magnitude of the resultant. **(2)**

(c) Given that the particle has mass 4 kg, find the magnitude of the acceleration of the particle, giving your answer to 3 decimal places. **(2)**

(d) Find the angle between the resultant and the unit vector **i** **(2)**

(Total 8 marks)

12. A particle is launched from the point P in a flat field, with velocity $31\,\text{m}\,\text{s}^{-1}$, at an angle of θ above the horizontal, as shown in the diagram.

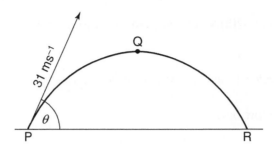

After 3 seconds, the particle reaches its maximum height, marked Q on the diagram.

(a) Show that $\sin \theta = 0.948$ to three significant figures. **(3)**

(b) Find the greatest height reached by the particle. **(3)**

(c) Find the horizontal distance between the launch point P and the landing point R **(3)**

(Total 9 marks)

13. A tractor of mass 3000 kg tows a trailer of mass 1500 kg in a straight line along a flat horizontal road. The tractor and trailer are connected by a light inextensible tow bar.

A horizontal driving force of 3200 N acts on the tractor and a horizontal resistance force of 900 N acts on the trailer.

The tractor and trailer accelerate at $0.5 \, \text{m s}^{-2}$. Assume the tow bar is horizontal.

(a) Find the tension in the tow bar. (3)

(b) Show that the magnitude of the horizontal resistance force on the tractor is 50 N. (4)

(Total 7 marks)

14. The displacement s of an object at time t seconds is given by the equation

$$s = 2t^3 - 5t^2 + 3t, \text{ where } t \geqslant 0$$

(a) Determine the displacement of the object after 6 seconds. (1)

(b) Find the velocity of the object when $t = 2$ (2)

(Total 3 marks)

15. A particle is moving in a plane.

At t seconds, its position r is given by $\mathbf{r} = (t^2 + 3)\mathbf{i} + (3t - 4)\mathbf{j}$, relative to the origin O

Find the speed of the particle and its direction of motion at $t = 4$ seconds.

(Total 7 marks)

16. A block is pulled up a rough plane inclined at an angle of $34°$ to the horizontal, as illustrated below.

The mass of the block is $1.2\,\text{kg}$ and the tension in the rope, which is parallel to the plane, is $T\,\text{N}$.

(a) Draw a diagram to model the forces acting on the block. **(1)**

(b) Work out the normal reaction force between the block and the plane. **(3)**

(c) Given that the coefficient of friction between the block and the plane is $\mu = 0.28$, find the magnitude of the frictional force acting on the block during its motion. **(2)**

(Total 6 marks)

Mathematics

Advanced Paper 1: Pure Mathematics 1   Time allowed: 2 hours

You must have:

Calculator

Mathematical Formulae (see pages 84–7)

Statistical Tables

Statistical tables are available on the Edexcel website. They can also be found on a calculator.

Candidates may use any calculator allowed by the regulations of the Joint Council for Qualifications. Calculators must not have the facility for symbolic algebra manipulation, differentiation and integration, or have retrievable mathematical formulae stored in them.

Instructions

- Use **black** ink or ball-point pen.
- If pencil is used for diagrams/sketches/graphs it must be dark (HB or B). Coloured pencils and highlighter pens must not be used.
- **Fill in the box** on the top of the page with your name.
- Answer **all** questions and ensure that your answers to parts of questions are clearly labelled.
- Answer the questions in the space provided after each question.
  - *if you require extra space please use a blank piece of paper.*
- You should show sufficient working to make your methods clear. Answers without working may not gain full credit.
- When a calculator is used, the answer should be given to an appropriate degree of accuracy.

Information

- The total mark for this paper is 100.
- The marks for **each** question are shown in brackets
  - *use this as a guide as to how much time to spend on each question.*

Advice

- Read each question carefully before you start to answer it.
- Try to answer every question.
- Check your answers if you have time at the end.

1. Find an approximation for $5\sin2\theta\cos2\theta$, when θ is small.

....

....

....

....

(Total 2 marks)

2. A circle C has equation $x^2 + y^2 - 6x + 2y - 15 = 0$

(a) Find the radius and the centre of the circle by completing the square. **(3)**

....

....

....

....

....

....

(b) (i) Using implicit differentiation to find the gradient, find the equation of the tangent to the circle at the point $(7, 2)$

Give your answer in the form $ax + by = c$ **(8)**

....

....

....

....

....

....

....

....

....

....

Question 2 continued

(ii) Find the equation of the normal to the circle at the same point. **(2)**

....

....

....

....

....

....

(Total 13 marks)

3. (a) Use the trapezium rule with 5 ordinates (4 strips) to estimate the value of $\int_0^1 \sqrt{x+1} \, \mathrm{d}x$

Give your answer to 4 significant figures. **(4)**

....

....

....

....

....

....

....

....

....

....

....

(b) Explain how you could find a more accurate estimate for the value of the integral using the trapezium rule. **(1)**

....

....

(Total 5 marks)

4. Simplify each of the following and hence show that all three expressions are equal.

(a) $\dfrac{\sqrt{50}}{5}$ **(1)**

....

....

....

(b) $7\sqrt{2} - \sqrt{72}$ **(1)**

....

....

....

(c) $\dfrac{\sqrt{22}}{\sqrt{11}}$ **(1)**

....

....

....

....

(Total 3 marks)

5. Sketch on separate diagrams for $0° \leqslant x \leqslant 360°$

(a) $y = 2\cos x$ **(2)**

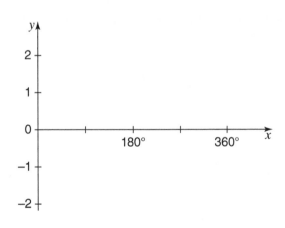

(b) $y = \cos 2x$ **(2)**

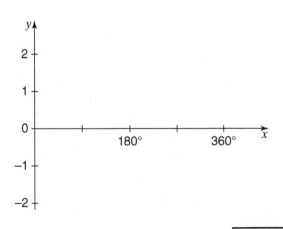

Question 5 continued

(c) $y = \cos(x + 30°)$ **(2)**

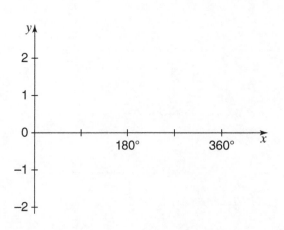

(Total 6 marks)

6. (a) Use the factor theorem to show that $x = 1$ is a solution of $f(x) = x^3 + 3x^2 - x - 3$ **(1)**

....

....

....

....

....

(b) By comparing coefficients, or otherwise, write $f(x)$ as a product of three linear factors. **(4)**

....

....

....

....

....

....

....

....

....

(Total 5 marks)

7. A curve has the equation $y = \dfrac{x+4}{1+x^2}$

(a) Show that $\dfrac{dy}{dx} = \dfrac{-x^2 - 8x + 1}{(1+x)^2}$ **(4)**

(b) Find the values of x for which the curve has stationary points. **(3)**

(Total 7 marks)

8. Sketch the graph of the equation $y = |x^2 - 3|$, clearly marking the intercepts on the axes.

(Total 3 marks)

9. Prove the identity $(\sin\theta + \csc\theta)^2 = \sin^2\theta + \cot^2\theta + 3$

(Total 3 marks)

10. Use the substitution $u = 3x + 1$ to find $\int x(3x + 1)^6 \, dx$. Give your answer in terms of x

(Total 4 marks)

11. Given that $\log_a x = 3(\log_a 4 - \log_a 2)$, where a is a positive constant, find x

(Total 3 marks)

12. The first term of an arithmetic series is 4 and the ninth term is four times the second term.

Find the sum of the first ten terms.

(Total 6 marks)

13. A circle, centre O, has radius 6cm. A chord intersects the circle at A and B, and AOB is in θ radians, where θ is acute.

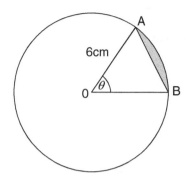

not accurately drawn

The area of the triangle AOB is 17.6 cm². Find:

(a) the angle θ,

(2)

....

....

....

....

....

....

(b) the area of the sector AOB,

(2)

....

....

....

....

....

....

(c) the area of the shaded segment.

(1)

....

....

(Total 5 marks)

14. (a) Functions f and g are defined as:

$$f(x) = 3x + 1, \ x \geqslant 0$$

$$g(x) = 2x^2, \ x \geqslant 0$$

Find the range of each of the following:

(i)   f(x)   **(1)**

(ii) g(x)   **(1)**

(iii) fg(x)   **(2)**

(b) (i) Find the inverse function $h^{-1}(x)$ given that $h(x) = \dfrac{1}{2x - 6}$ **(3)**

(ii) State the domain of $h^{-1}(x)$ **(1)**

(Total 8 marks)

15. (a) Find $\int \frac{\cos x}{\sin x} \, \mathrm{d}x$ **(2)**

(b) Find $\int \frac{4x}{4x^2 + 3} \, \mathrm{d}x$ **(3)**

(Total 5 marks)

16. (a) Find the general solution of the differential equation

$$\frac{1}{x} \frac{\mathrm{d}y}{\mathrm{d}x} = \frac{1}{x^2 + 1}$$ **(3)**

(b) Find the particular solution of the differential equation that passes through the point $(3, 2)$ **(2)**

(Total 5 marks)

17. (a) Express $5\cos x - 3\sin x$ in the form $R\cos(x + \alpha)$, where $R > 0$ and $0° \leqslant x \leqslant 360°$

Give R in surd form and α to the nearest degree. **(5)**

(b) Hence solve the equation $5\cos x - 3\sin x = 2$ in the interval $0° \leqslant x \leqslant 360°$

Give your answer to the nearest $0.1°$ **(4)**

(Total 9 marks)

18. Give a counter example to disprove each of the following statements:

(a) For every prime number p, $2p + 1$ is prime. **(2)**

(b) If a and b are irrational real numbers, their product ab is also irrational. **(2)**

(Total 4 marks)

19. The first four terms in the binomial expansion $\left(1 + \dfrac{x}{2}\right)^4$ are $1 + ax + bx^2 + cx^3$

Find the values of the constants a, b and c, giving your answers in their simplest form.

(Total 4 marks)

Name: ....

Mathematics

Advanced Paper 2: Pure Mathematics 2   Time allowed: 2 hours

You must have:

Calculator

Mathematical Formulae (see pages 84–7)

Statistical Tables

Statistical tables are available on the Edexcel website. They can also be found on a calculator.

Candidates may use any calculator allowed by the regulations of the Joint Council for Qualifications. Calculators must not have the facility for symbolic algebra manipulation, differentiation and integration, or have retrievable mathematical formulae stored in them.

Instructions

- Use **black** ink or ball-point pen.
- If pencil is used for diagrams/sketches/graphs it must be dark (HB or B). Coloured pencils and highlighter pens must not be used.
- **Fill in the box** on the top of the page with your name.
- Answer **all** questions and ensure that your answers to parts of questions are clearly labelled.
- Answer the questions in the space provided after each question.
  - *if you require extra space please use a blank piece of paper.*
- You should show sufficient working to make your methods clear. Answers without working may not gain full credit.
- When a calculator is used, the answer should be given to an appropriate degree of accuracy.

Information

- The total mark for this paper is 100.
- The marks for **each** question are shown in brackets
  - *use this as a guide as to how much time to spend on each question.*

Advice

- Read each question carefully before you start to answer it.
- Try to answer every question.
- Check your answers if you have time at the end.

1. Solve the inequality $3(2 - 2x) \geqslant 4(x + 2)$

(Total 1 mark)

2. Determine the derivative of $y = -5e^{3x-1}$

(Total 2 marks)

3. A triangle has sides a = 7 cm, b = 4 cm and c = 5 cm.

Use the cosine rule to find the angle A that lies between sides b and c, giving your answer in degrees.

(Total 1 mark)

4. The straight line $y = x - 1$ intersects the circle $x^2 + y^2 = 25$ at the points M and N.

(a) Show that the x-coordinates of the points M and N satisfy the equation $x^2 - x - 12 = 0$ **(3)**

(b) Hence find the coordinates of M and N. **(3)**

(Total 6 marks)

5. A curve is defined parametrically by $x = 3t^2 + 4t + 1$ and $y = t^3 + t^2$

Find $\dfrac{dy}{dx}$ terms of t

(Total 4 marks)

6. Find the exact value of

$$\int_{-\frac{\pi}{4}}^{\frac{\pi}{4}} \frac{\sin^2 x}{3}\, dx$$

(Total 6 marks)

7. (a) Find the sum to infinity of the geometric series $\frac{1}{2} - \frac{1}{4} + \frac{1}{8} - \ldots$ **(4)**

(b) Find the common ratio r of a geometric series which has a first term of 5 and $S_\infty = 6$ **(3)**

(Total 7 marks)

8. Newton's Law of Cooling states that the rate of change of the temperature T of an object is proportional to the difference between its own temperature and the temperature of its surroundings. An object at 74°C is placed in a room with a temperature of 16°C and after 5 minutes it has cooled to 62°C.

(a) Write down the differential equation to model this situation. **(2)**

(b) Use separation of variables to show that a formula for the temperature T is given by

$$T = e^c \times e^{-kt}$$

(4)

Question 8 continued

(c) By calculating the value for e^c, work out the temperature of the object after a further 5 minutes.

(6)

....

....

....

....

....

....

....

....

....

....

....

....

....

....

....

....

....

(Total 12 marks)

9. The equation $e^{2x} + 4x - 5 = 0$ has one real root α.

(a) Show that α lies between 0 and 1 **(2)**

(b) Using $x_1 = 0.5$ as a first approximation to α, apply the Newton-Raphson method to find a second approximation, x_2, to α

Give your answer to 5 decimal places. **(4)**

(Total 6 marks)

10. Two particles M and N have position vectors $\mathbf{m} = (3\mathbf{i} - 4\mathbf{j})$ and $\mathbf{n} = (6\mathbf{i} + 2\mathbf{j})$ relative to the origin O. Particle M is displaced by $(3\mathbf{i} + 6\mathbf{j})$ and particle N moves in the direction of $\mathbf{n}$ to twice its original distance from O

(a) Find the position vectors of M and N after displacement and calculate the new distance between them, giving your answer in exact form. **(4)**

(b) Using your answer to part (a), show that M, N and a third particle P with position vector $\mathbf{p} = (15\mathbf{i} + 5\mathbf{j})$ are now collinear. **(3)**

(Total 7 marks)

11. Find an approximation for each of the following expressions when θ is very small.

(a) $\cos \theta + 3\sin \theta$ **(1)**

(b) $\dfrac{3\tan \theta - \theta}{\sin 2\theta}$ **(2)**

(c) $\cot \theta (1 - \cos \theta)$ **(3)**

(d) $\dfrac{\sqrt{3} - \sin \theta}{\cos \theta}$ **(3)**

(Total 9 marks)

12. (a) Express $\dfrac{3}{(2x+1)(x-1)}$ in the form $\dfrac{A}{(2x+1)} + \dfrac{B}{(x-1)}$, where A and B are integers. **(3)**

(b) Hence find $\displaystyle\int_2^3 \dfrac{3}{(2x+1)(x-1)}$, leaving your answer in exact form. **(4)**

(Total 7 marks)

13. For the curve $y = x^3 + 6x^2 + 12x + 12$, find the coordinates of the stationary points and state their nature.

(Total 7 marks)

14. By using a suitable trigonometric identity, solve $2\sec^2\theta - 3 + \tan\theta = 0$

Give all solutions in the range $0° \leqslant x \leqslant 360°$

(Total 6 marks)

15. Prove that a three-digit number is divisible by 3 if the sum of its digits is divisible by 3. Use a, b and c as the three digits.

(Total 7 marks)

16. A curve has equation $f(x) = 4x^2 - 5x + 2$

   (a) Use differentiation from first principles to find $f'(x)$ **(6)**

   (b) Hence determine the values of x for which the function is increasing. **(2)**

16. A curve has equation $f(x) = 4x^2 - 5x + 2$

   (a) Use differentiation from first principles to find $f'(x)$

(Total 8 marks)

17. Differentiate each of the following with respect to x

(a) $y = \cos(6x - 5)$ **(2)**

(b) $y = \ln(x^3 - 5x + 1)$ **(2)**

(Total 4 marks)

Mathematics

Advanced Paper 3: Statistics and Mechanics

Time allowed: 2 hours

You must have:

Calculator

Mathematical Formulae (see pages 84–7)

Statistical Tables

Statistical tables are available on the Edexcel website. They can also be found on a calculator.

Candidates may use any calculator allowed by the regulations of the Joint Council for Qualifications. Calculators must not have the facility for symbolic algebra manipulation, differentiation and integration, or have retrievable mathematical formulae stored in them.

Instructions

- Use **black** ink or ball-point pen.
- If pencil is used for diagrams/sketches/graphs it must be dark (HB or B). Coloured pencils and highlighter pens must not be used.
- **Fill in the box** on the top of the page with your name.
- Answer **all** questions and ensure that your answers to parts of questions are clearly labelled.
- Answer the questions in the space provided after each question.
  – *if you require extra space please use a blank piece of paper.*
- You should show sufficient working to make your methods clear. Answers without working may not gain full credit.
- When a calculator is used, the answer should be given to an appropriate degree of accuracy.

Information

- The total mark for this paper is 100.
- The marks for **each** question are shown in brackets
  – *use this as a guide as to how much time to spend on each question.*

Advice

- Read each question carefully before you start to answer it.
- Try to answer every question.
- Check your answers if you have time at the end.

SECTION A : STATISTICS

1. Tim, Jude and Kris each have a set of game cards. Each set of cards contains an identical mixture of red, green and silver cards. Each person chooses one card from their set.

    The table shows the probabilities of each person choosing the different types of card. All the events are independent.

	Red card	Green card	Silver card
Tim	0.25	0.65	0.10
Jude	0.15	0.40	0.45
Kris	0.20	0.25	0.55

    (a) Calculate the probabilities that:

        (i) each person chooses a red card   **(2)**

        (ii) only Tim chooses a green card   **(2)**

        (iii) at least two of Tim, Jude and Kris choose a silver card.   **(4)**

Kellie, Kris's sister, has a set of the same cards. She removes all the red cards from her set.

The probability that Kellie chooses a green card, given that Kris chooses green is 0.8

The probability that Kellie chooses a silver card, given that Kris chooses silver is 0.6

(b) Calculate the probability that Kris and Kellie choose:

(i) the same type of card, (3)

(ii) different types of card. (1)

(Total 12 marks)

2. The time given to students to complete an exam is 120 minutes.

The time taken for students to complete the exam follows a normal distribution with a mean of 100 minutes and a standard deviation of 5.9 minutes.

(a) Find the probability that a student takes longer than 110 minutes to complete the exam. (3)

(b) Find the probability that a student completes the exam in under 92 minutes. (2)

Jamie claims that he has perfected his timing to within 95 and 105 minutes so that he has time left to check over his exam.

(c) Calculate the probability that he will complete the exam within this time frame. (1)

(Total 6 marks)

3. The three scatter diagrams A, B and C below show the daily mean temperature in °C for June and July, in 1987 and 2015, in three different locations taken from the Large Data Set.

A – Daily mean temperature, °C

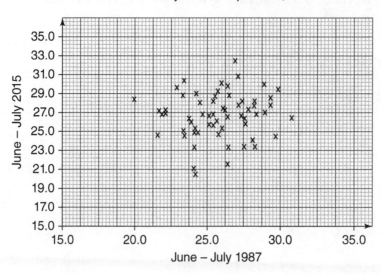

June – July 1987

B – Daily mean temperature, °C

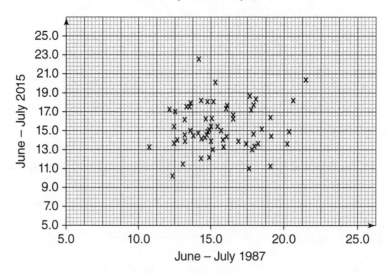

June – July 1987

C – Daily mean temperature, °C

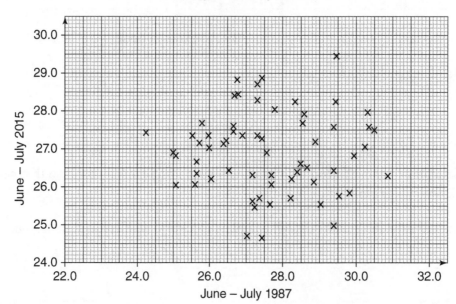

June – July 1987

(a) Using your knowledge of the large data set, or otherwise, suggest the location each scatter diagram A, B, C represents, choosing from the following list: Beijing, Leeming, Perth, Jacksonville and Camborne. **(2)**

(b) The daily mean temperature, °C, for Camborne in October 1987 can be modelled by N $(10.79, 2.14^2)$

   (i) Calculate how many days you would expect the daily mean temperature to be between 10 and 12°C **(2)**

   (ii) Calculate how many days you would expect the daily mean temperature to be below the mean by at least one standard deviation. **(2)**

(Total 6 marks)

4. A manufacturer claims that the lifetime of its AA batteries is normally distributed with a mean of 1320 minutes and a standard deviation of 26.4 minutes. Ruth suspects that the batteries do not last as long as the manufacturer claims, as she finds that they run out much quicker than this. She tests a random sample of six AA batteries in her torch and finds that their lifetimes are 1242, 1356, 1195, 1287, 1306 and 1394 minutes.

(a) Carry out a hypothesis test at the 1% significance level, to investigate whether the AA batteries last less time than the manufacturer claims. **(5)**

(b) Calculate the smallest sample mean length of battery life that would have resulted in Ruth coming to a different conclusion than your answer to part (a) **(2)**

(Total 7 marks)

5. Mark is collecting data about visibility at Heathrow. He wants to take a random sample of size 30 from data recorded in 1987.

(a) Write down the steps Mark should take to do this. **(2)**

Mark calculates the following for visibility at Heathrow:

$$\sum x = 63800 \qquad \frac{\sum (x - \bar{x})^2}{n} = 833747$$

(b) Work out the mean and standard deviation for visibility at Heathrow. **(2)**

(c) Use your knowledge of the large data set to explain in context your answer to part (b) **(1)**

(Total 5 marks)

6. Micheal, a maths teacher, catches the bus to school each day. The time the bus arrives is not dependent on the day, or on the time it arrived on other days.

Micheal claims that the probability his bus arrives on time is 0.45

(a) Assuming his claim is true, find the probability that his bus arrives on time:

   (i) on at most 7 days during a 3-week period (15 school days), **(2)**

   (ii) on more than 12 but fewer than 18 days during a half term (6 weeks). **(3)**

(b) Assuming his claim is true, calculate the mean and standard deviation for the number of times in one week that Micheal's bus arrives on time. **(3)**

(c) Micheal's colleague Jonathan catches the same bus as Micheal for 10 weeks. He records the number of times their bus is on time each week. His results are:

3   1   2   4   0   1   3   2   2   3

(i) Calculate the mean and standard deviation of these values. **(3)**

(ii) Hence comment on the validity of Micheal's claim. **(2)**

(Total 13 marks)

SECTION B : MECHANICS

7. A horizontal force H acts on a particle of mass 9 kg, which is at rest on a rough horizontal plane.

The coefficient of friction μ between the particle and the plane is 0.3
Find the range of values of the frictional force F

....

....

....

....

(Total 2 marks)

8. The displacement of a toy fire engine as it travels across a playground can be described by the equation $s = 0.4 + 1.4t^2 - 0.1t^3$, where s is its displacement from a bench after t seconds.

(a) Find the velocity of the fire engine after 6 seconds. **(2)**

....

....

....

(b) Find the acceleration after 6 seconds. **(2)**

....

....

....

(c) Find the initial displacement of the fire engine from the bench. **(1)**

....

....

(d) Find the average velocity of the fire engine during the first 6 seconds of its motion. **(2)**

....

....

....

(Total 7 marks)

9. A PE teacher pulls a crate of basketballs across the floor of a gym using a horizontal rope. The mass of the crate is 23 kg. The crate moves with a constant acceleration of 0.8 m s⁻² and the frictional force between the floor and the crate is 11 N.

(a) Draw a force diagram to show this situation. **(2)**

(b) Find the tension in the rope. **(3)**

....

....

....

....

....

....

(Total 5 marks)

10. A dog runs in a straight line after its ball, at a constant speed of 5.8 m s⁻¹. After 6 seconds, it sees a bird and accelerates with a constant acceleration of 1.44 m s⁻² for 5 seconds. The dog then gets tired and slows down, decelerating uniformly for 3 seconds before it comes to a stop and lies down.

(a) Sketch a velocity time graph to model this situation. **(3)**

(b) Find the deceleration of the dog when it slows down. **(1)**

....

....

Question 10 continued

(c) Find the total distance travelled by the dog. **(3)**

....

....

....

....

....

(Total 7 marks)

11. A drone moves through the air with acceleration $(5\mathbf{i} - 11\mathbf{j})\,\mathrm{m\,s^{-2}}$

Initially its velocity is $3\mathbf{i}\,\mathrm{m\,s^{-1}}$. The drone can be modelled as a particle.

(a) Find the velocity of the drone at time t **(2)**

....

....

....

....

(b) Find its speed when $t = 1.5$ seconds. **(3)**

....

....

....

....

....

(Total 5 marks)

12. Two particles of mass $4\,\mathrm{kg}$ and $5\,\mathrm{kg}$ are connected by a light inextensible string passing over a smooth fixed pulley. The $4\,\mathrm{kg}$ mass is at rest on a rough horizontal plane, with $\mu = 0.3$, and the $5\,\mathrm{kg}$ mass hangs vertically below the pulley.

(a) Draw a diagram to show the forces acting on the $4\,\mathrm{kg}$ mass. **(1)**

(b) Determine the acceleration of both particles immediately after they are released from rest. **(5)**

(c) Calculate the magnitude of the tension in the string. **(2)**

A horizontal force, P, acts on the 4 kg mass, such that the system is in limiting equilibrium and the 5 kg mass is on the point of moving upwards.

(d) Find the magnitude of force, P. **(3)**

(Total 11 marks)

13. A uniform bar, PQ, of length 5 m and mass 4 kg is suspended in a horizontal position by two vertical strings at points P and Q. A bird table of mass 2 kg hangs from the bar, 1.25 m from P.

(a) Sketch a force diagram to model this situation.

(2)

(b) Find the tensions in the two strings, T_P and T_Q

(5)

(Total 7 marks)

14. A particle is projected from a point which is 2 m above ground level with an initial velocity of 40 m s⁻¹ at an angle of 45° to the horizontal.

(a) Find the horizontal distance travelled when it hits the ground. **(5)**

A second particle is projected from ground level with the same velocity and at the same angle as the first particle.

(b) Show that the second particle takes 0.07 seconds less than the first particle to hit the ground. **(2)**

(Total 7 marks)

Formulae

Pure Mathematics

Mensuration

Surface area of sphere = $4\pi r^2$

Area of curved surface of cone = $\pi r \times$ slant height

Arithmetic series

$$S_n = \frac{1}{2}n(a + l) = \frac{1}{2}n[2a + (n-1)d]$$

Binomial series

$$(a + b)^n = a^n + \binom{n}{1}a^{n-1}b + \binom{n}{2}a^{n-2}b^2 + \dots + \binom{n}{r}a^{n-r}b^r + \dots + b^n \quad (n \in \mathbb{N})$$

$$\text{Where } \binom{n}{r} = {}^nC_r = \frac{n!}{r!(n-r)!}$$

$$(1 + x)^n = 1 + nx + \frac{n(n-1)}{1 \times 2}x^2 + \dots + \frac{n(n-1)\dots(n-r+1)}{1 \times 2 \times \dots \times r}x^r + \dots \quad \left(|x| < 1, n \in \mathbb{R}\right)$$

Logarithms and exponentials

$$\log_a x = \frac{\log_b x}{\log_b a}$$

$$e^{x\ln a} = a^x$$

Geometric series

$$S_n = \frac{a\left(1 - r^n\right)}{1 - r}$$

$$S_\infty = \frac{a}{1 - r} \text{ for } |r| < 1$$

Trigonometric identities

$$\sin(A \pm B) = \sin A \cos B \pm \cos A \sin B$$

$$\cos(A \pm B) = \cos A \cos B \mp \sin A \sin B$$

$$\tan(A \pm B) = \frac{\tan A \pm \tan B}{1 \mp \tan A \tan B} \quad \left(A \pm B \neq \left(k + \frac{1}{2}\right)\pi\right)$$

$$\sin A + \sin B = 2\sin\frac{A + B}{2}\cos\frac{A - B}{2}$$

$$\sin A - \sin B = 2\cos\frac{A + B}{2}\sin\frac{A - B}{2}$$

$$\cos A + \cos B = 2\cos\frac{A + B}{2}\cos\frac{A - B}{2}$$

$$\cos A - \cos B = -2\sin\frac{A + B}{2}\sin\frac{A - B}{2}$$

Small angle approximations

$\sin\theta \approx \theta$

$\cos\theta \approx 1 - \dfrac{\theta^2}{2}$

$\tan\theta \approx \theta$

where θ is measured in radians

Differentiation

First Principles

$$f'(x) = \lim_{h\to 0}\frac{f(x+h)-f(x)}{h}$$

$f(x)$	$f'(x)$
$\tan kx$	$k\sec^2 kx$
$\sec kx$	$k\sec kx\tan kx$
$\cot kx$	$-k\operatorname{cosec}^2 kx$
$\operatorname{cosec} kx$	$-k\operatorname{cosec} kx\cot kx$
$\dfrac{f(x)}{g(x)}$	$\dfrac{f'(x)g(x)-f(x)g'(x)}{\left(g(x)\right)^2}$

Integration	**(+ constant)**
$f(x)$	$\int f(x)\,dx$
$\sec^2 kx$	$\dfrac{1}{k}\tan kx$
$\tan kx$	$\dfrac{1}{k}\ln\lvert\sec kx\rvert$
$\cot kx$	$\dfrac{1}{k}\ln\lvert\sin kx\rvert$
$\operatorname{cosec} kx$	$-\dfrac{1}{k}\ln\lvert\operatorname{cosec} kx + \cot kx\rvert,\quad \dfrac{1}{k}\ln\left\lvert\tan\left(\dfrac{1}{2}kx\right)\right\rvert$
$\sec kx$	$\dfrac{1}{k}\ln\lvert\sec kx + \tan kx\rvert,\quad \dfrac{1}{k}\ln\left\lvert\tan\left(\dfrac{1}{2}kx + \dfrac{1}{4}\pi\right)\right\rvert$

$$\int u\frac{dv}{dx}\,dx = uv - \int v\frac{du}{dx}\,dx$$

Numerical Methods

The trapezium rule: $\int_a^b y\,dx \approx \dfrac{1}{2}h\left\{(y_0 + y_n) + 2(y_1 + y_2 + \ldots + y_{n-1})\right\}$, where $h = \dfrac{b-a}{n}$

The Newton-Raphson iteration for solving $f(x)=0$: $x_{n+1} = x_n - \dfrac{f(x_n)}{f'(x_n)}$

Statistics

Probability

$P(A') = 1 - P(A)$

$P(A \cup B) = P(A) + P(B) - P(A \cap B)$

$P(A \cap B) = P(A)P(B|A)$

$P(A|B) = \dfrac{P(B|A)P(A)}{P(B|A)P(A) + P(B|A')P(A')}$

For independent events A and B,

$P(B|A) = P(B)$

$P(A|B) = P(A)$

$P(A \cap B) = P(A)P(B)$

Standard deviation

Standard deviation $= \sqrt{(\text{Variance})}$

Interquartile range $= \text{IQR} = Q_3 - Q_1$

For a set of n values $x_1, x_2, \ldots x_i, \ldots x_n$

$S_{xx} = \sum\left(x_i - \bar{x}\right)^2 = \sum x_i^2 - \dfrac{\left(\sum x_i\right)^2}{n}$

Standard deviation $= \sqrt{\dfrac{S_{xx}}{n}}$ or $\sqrt{\dfrac{\sum x^2}{n} - \bar{x}^2}$

Discrete distributions

Distribution of X	$P(X=x)$	Mean	Variance
Binomial B(n, p)	$\dbinom{n}{x}p^x\left(1-p\right)^{n-x}$	np	$np(1-p)$

Sampling distributions

For a random sample of n observations from $N(\mu, \sigma^2)$

$\dfrac{\bar{X} - \mu}{\dfrac{\sigma}{\sqrt{n}}} \sim N(0,1)$

Statistical tables

The following statistical tables are required for A Level Mathematics:

Binomial Cumulative Distribution Function

Percentage Points of The Normal Distribution

Critical Values for Correlation Coefficients: Product Moment Coefficient

Random Numbers

Mechanics

Kinematics

For motion in a straight line with constant acceleration:

$v = u + at$

$s = ut + \dfrac{1}{2}at^2$

$s = vt + \dfrac{1}{2}at^2$

$v^2 = u^2 + 2as$

$s = \dfrac{1}{2}(u + v)t$

Answers

EDEXCEL ANSWERS

Guidance on marking your own answers.

Where the correct final answer is given without clear method shown, only the final mark should be awarded.

There is often more than one way to solve a problem. Students should not automatically discount their solution if it is different to the one shown: check with a teacher instead.

SET 1 PAPER 1

1. $u_1 = ar^{n-1} = ar^0 = 30 \times 1 = 30, \therefore a = 30; u_2 = ar^{n-1} = ar^1 = 18,$
   $30 \times r = 18 \Rightarrow r = \dfrac{18}{30} = 0.6$ **(2)**

2. $m = 5$ so m of perpendicular line is $-\dfrac{1}{m} = -\dfrac{1}{5}$.

   $y - y_1 = m(x - x_1)$ using $m = -\dfrac{1}{5}$ and point $(2, 7)$ **(1)**

   $y - 7 = -\dfrac{1}{5}(x - 2) \Rightarrow 5y - 35 = -1(x - 2)$
   $\Rightarrow 5y - 35 = -x + 2 \Rightarrow 5y + x = 37$ **(1)**

3. **(a)** $\sqrt{27} = \sqrt{3} \times \sqrt{9}$, $\sqrt{3} \times \sqrt{9} = 3\sqrt{3}$, $3\sqrt{3} = 3^{\frac{3}{2}}$ **(1)**;
   $3^m = 3^{\frac{3}{2}}, \therefore m = \dfrac{3}{2}$ or 1.5 **(1)**

   (b) $\sqrt{27} = 3^{\frac{3}{2}}$, $3^{\frac{3}{2}} = 3^{2x}$
   $\therefore 2x = \dfrac{3}{2}$, $x = \dfrac{3}{2} \div 2$, $x = \dfrac{3}{5}$ or 0.75 **(1)**

4. **(a)** stretch in the y-direction **(1)**, scale factor 3 **(1)**
   (b) translation **(1)** in the (–ve) x-direction by 45° **(1)**
   (or by –45° if negative direction not stated)
   (c) reflection **(1)** in the x-axis **(1)**

5.
n	$n^2 + 1$
8	$65 = 3 \times 21 + 2, \therefore$ not divisible by 3
9	$82 = 3 \times 27 + 1, \therefore$ not divisible by 3
10	$101 = 3 \times 33 + 2, \therefore$ not divisible by 3
11	$122 = 3 \times 40 + 2, \therefore$ not divisible by 3
12	$145 = 3 \times 48 + 1, \therefore$ not divisible by 3

   (3) for all lines correct, or **(1)** for 4 correct $n^2 + 1$ values and **(1)** for explanation
   $\therefore n^2 + 1$ is not divisible by 3 for $8 \le n \le 12$ **(1)**

6. $u = 1, \dfrac{du}{d\theta} = 0, v = \cos\theta, \dfrac{dv}{d\theta} = -\sin\theta.$

   Using $\dfrac{v\dfrac{du}{d\theta} - u\dfrac{dv}{d\theta}}{v^2}$, $\dfrac{dx}{d\theta} = \dfrac{-(-\sin\theta)}{(\cos\theta)^2}$ **(1)**

   $\dfrac{dx}{d\theta} = \dfrac{\sin\theta}{\cos^2\theta}$;

   $\dfrac{\sin\theta}{\cos\theta \times \cos\theta} = \tan\theta \times \dfrac{1}{\cos\theta}$ **(1)** $= \tan\theta \sec\theta$ **(1)**

7. $1 + 3x + \dfrac{3(3-1)}{1 \times 2}x^2 + \dfrac{3(3-1)(3-1)}{1 \times 2 \times 3}x^3$ **(1)**

   $\Rightarrow 1 + 3x + \dfrac{6}{2}x^2 + \dfrac{6}{6}x^3$ **(1)** $\Rightarrow 1 + 3x + 3x^2 + x^3$ **(1)**

8. Chain rule: $\dfrac{dy}{dx} = \dfrac{dy}{du} \times \dfrac{du}{dx}$

   (a) $u = 4x + 1, y = u^3, \dfrac{du}{dx} = 4, \dfrac{dy}{du} = 3u^2$ **(1)**

   $\dfrac{dy}{dx} = 12u^2 = 12(4x + 1)^2$ **(1)**

   (b) $u = 4x + 1, y = \ln u, \dfrac{du}{dx} = 4, \dfrac{dy}{du} = \dfrac{1}{u}, \dfrac{dy}{dx} = \dfrac{4}{u}$ **(1)**

   $\dfrac{dy}{dx} = \dfrac{4}{4x + 1}$ **(1)**

   (c) Product rule: $\dfrac{dy}{dx} = u\dfrac{dv}{dx} + v\dfrac{du}{dx}$; $u = (4x + 1)^3$ and $v = \ln(4x + 1)$;
   $\dfrac{du}{dx} = 12(4x + 1)^2$ (from (a)), $\dfrac{dv}{dx} = \dfrac{4}{4x + 1}$ (from (b))
   $\dfrac{dy}{dx} = (4x + 1)^3 \times \dfrac{4}{4x + 1} + \ln(4x + 1) \times 12(4x + 1)^2$ **(1)**
   $4(4x + 1)^2 + 12(4x + 1)^2 \ln(4x + 1)$ **(1)**
   $= 4(4x + 1)^2(1 + 3\ln(4x + 1))$ **(1)**

9. **(a)** $\dfrac{5 + \sqrt{3}}{3 + \sqrt{3}} \times \dfrac{3 - \sqrt{3}}{3 - \sqrt{3}}$ **(1)** $= \dfrac{15 - 5\sqrt{3} + 3\sqrt{3} - 3}{9 - 3\sqrt{3} + 3\sqrt{3} - 3}$ **(1)**
   $= \dfrac{12 - 2\sqrt{3}}{6} = \dfrac{6 - \sqrt{3}}{3} \therefore (m =)\, 6$ **(1)**, $(n =)\, 3$ **(1)**

   (b) $\sqrt{32} = 4\sqrt{2}$ **(1)**, $\dfrac{10}{\sqrt{2}} \times \dfrac{\sqrt{2}}{\sqrt{2}} = \dfrac{10\sqrt{2}}{2} = 5\sqrt{2}$ **(1)**;
   $4\sqrt{2} + 5\sqrt{2} = 9\sqrt{2}$ **(1)**

10. **(a)** $f(x) \ge 0$ **(2)** or **(1)** if $x \ge 0$, $f(x) > 0$
    (b) (i) $y = \sqrt{2x + 4}$, exchange x and y, $x = \sqrt{2y + 4}$ **(1)**,
    $x^2 = 2y + 4, 2y = x^2 - 4$ **(1)** $y = \dfrac{1}{2}(x^2 - 4)$.
    $f^{-1}(x) = \dfrac{1}{2}(x^2 - 4)$ **(1)**

    (ii) Range of a function = domain of its inverse,
    $\therefore$ domain of f^{-1} is $x \ge 0$ **(1)**

    (c) (i) $h(x) = fg(x) = \sqrt{2\left(\dfrac{1}{2x + 1}\right) + 4}$ **(2)**

    (ii) $\sqrt{2\left(\dfrac{1}{2x + 1}\right) + 4} = 4$ **(1)** $\Rightarrow 2\left(\dfrac{1}{2x + 1}\right) + 4 = 16$ **(1)**
    $\Rightarrow x = \dfrac{-5}{12}$ **(1)**

11. **(a)** area $= \dfrac{1}{2}ab\sin C \Rightarrow \dfrac{1}{2} \times 10 \times 11 \times \dfrac{4}{5}$ **(1)** $= 44\text{m}^2$ **(1)**

    (b) $\sin\theta = \dfrac{4}{5} = \dfrac{\text{opp}}{\text{hyp}}$, Pythagoras: $\text{adj}^2 = \text{hyp}^2 - \text{opp}^2$
    $\Rightarrow \text{adj}^2 = 5^2 - 4^2$, $\text{adj} = \sqrt{9} = 3$. $\cos\theta = \dfrac{3}{5} = 0.6$ **(1)**

    (c) Cosine rule. $PR^2 = 10^2 + 11^2 - 2 \times 10 \times 11 \times \dfrac{3}{5} = 89$
    (1); $PR = \sqrt{89}$ **(1)** $= 9.43$ to 3 s.f. **(1)**

Answers

12. (a) $V = 15000 \times 1.2^{-4}$ **(1)** $= £7233.80 \approx £7234$ **(1)**

(b) $15000 \times (1.2)^{-t}$ **(1)** < 4000 **(1)**; $1.2^{-t} < \dfrac{4000}{15000}$;

$\ln 1.2^{-t} < \ln\left(\dfrac{4000}{15000}\right)$ **(1)**; $-t \ln 1.2 < \ln\left(\dfrac{4000}{15000}\right)$;

$-t < \dfrac{\ln\left(\dfrac{4000}{15000}\right)}{\ln 1.2}$ **(1)**; $t > \dfrac{-\ln\left(\dfrac{4000}{15000}\right)}{\ln 1.2}$;

$t > 7.25$ years **(1)**

(c) After 7 years and 3 months, the car's value drops below £4000 **(1)**

13. (a) ① $-2 - \lambda = 0 - \mu$; ② $10 + 3\lambda = 8 - \mu$;

③ $4 + 2\lambda = 1 + \mu$ **(1)**

Solving the first pair of simultaneous equations:

① $\mu - \lambda = 2$ and ② $\mu + 3\lambda = -2$ **(1)**

Subtracting ② from ① gives $-4\lambda = 4$, $\lambda = -1$

hence $\mu = 1$ **(1)**.

Substituting these values for λ and μ gives the same point of intersection ∴ the lines intersect. **(1)** ∴ $P = (-1, 7, 2)$ **(1)**

(b) $\begin{pmatrix} 0 \\ 8 \\ 1 \end{pmatrix} + \mu \begin{pmatrix} -1 \\ -1 \\ 1 \end{pmatrix} = \begin{pmatrix} -3 \\ 5 \\ 4 \end{pmatrix}$ **(1)**; $0 - \mu = -3, \mu = 3$; $8 - \mu = 5, \mu = 3$;

$1 + \mu = 4, \mu = 3$ ∴ point lies on line **(1)**

14. (a) By factor theorem, if $(x - 2)$ is a factor, $f(x) = 0$; $f(2) = 3(2^3)$ $+ 2(2^2) - 19(2) + k = 0$ **(1)** $\Rightarrow -6 + k = 0 \Rightarrow k = 6$ **(1)**

(b) $(x - 2)(ax^2 + bx + c) = 3x^3 + 2x^2 - 19x + 6$; $ax^3 + bx^2 +$ $cx - 2ax^2 - 2bx - 2c = 3x^3 + 2x^2 - 19x + 6$ **(1)**;

Equating coefficients, $a = 3$, $b = 8$, $c = -3$ **(1)**

$(x - 2)(3x^2 + 8x - 3) = (x - 2)(3x - 1)(x + 3)$ as required **(1)**

15. (a) $\dfrac{3}{x^2 - x - 2} = \dfrac{A}{x + 1} + \dfrac{B}{x - 2}$; adding fractions gives

$\dfrac{A(x - 2) + B(x + 1)}{(x + 1)(x - 2)}$ **(1)**.

Equating both sides, $A = -1$, $B = 1$ **(2)**

∴ $\dfrac{3}{x^2 - x - 2} = \dfrac{-1}{x + 1} + \dfrac{1}{x - 2}$ as required **(1)**

(b) $3 \int \dfrac{1}{x - 2} - \dfrac{-1}{x + 1} \, dx$ **(1)** $= 3 \left[\ln|x - 2| + \ln|x + 1| \right] (+c)$ **(1)**

$= 3 \ln \dfrac{x - 2}{x + 1} (+c)$ **(1)**

16. Let $u = 2x + 1$ **(1)**, $\dfrac{du}{dx} = 2$, $dx = \dfrac{du}{2}$, $x = \dfrac{(u - 1)}{2}$;

New limits $u = 2 \times 1 + 1 = 3$ and $u = 2 \times 0 + 1 = 1$ **(1)**;

$\int_1^3 \left(\dfrac{u - 1}{2}\right) u^{\frac{1}{2}} \dfrac{du}{2}$ **(1)**

$\dfrac{1}{4} \int_1^3 u^{\frac{3}{2}} - u^{\frac{1}{2}} \, du$ **(1)** $\Rightarrow \dfrac{1}{4} \left[\dfrac{u^{\frac{5}{2}}}{\frac{5}{2}} - \dfrac{u^{\frac{3}{2}}}{\frac{3}{2}} \right] \Rightarrow \dfrac{1}{4} \left[\dfrac{2u^{\frac{5}{2}}}{5} - \dfrac{2u^{\frac{3}{2}}}{2} \right]$ **(1)**

$\Rightarrow \dfrac{1}{4} \left[\left(\dfrac{2 \times 3^{\frac{5}{2}}}{5} - \dfrac{2 \times 3^{\frac{3}{2}}}{3} \right) - \left(\dfrac{2 \times 1^{\frac{5}{2}}}{5} - \dfrac{2 \times 1^{\frac{3}{2}}}{3} \right) \right]$ **(1)**

$\Rightarrow \dfrac{1 + 6\sqrt{3}}{15}$ **(1)**

17. (a) (i) centre C is $(8, 15)$ **(1)**; **(ii)** radius $= \sqrt{289} = 17$ **(1)**

(b) (i) sub $x = 0$ and $y = 0$ into equation of circle.

$8^2 + 15^2 = 289$ **(1)**

(ii) Sub $x = 0$ into equation and rearrange to get

$y^2 - 30y = 0$; $y(y - 30) = 0$ so $y = 0$ or $y = 30$, ∴ $p = 30$ **(1)**

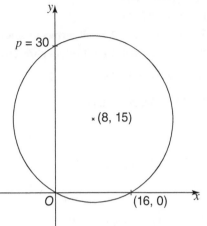

(1 for correct diagram)

18. (a) (1 for fully correct diagram)

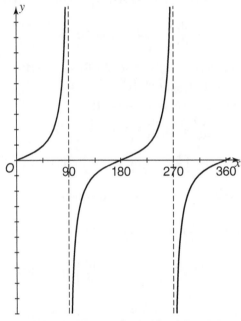

(b) $\theta = \tan^{-1} 1.327 = 53°$, ∴ $53° + 180° = 233°$; $\theta = 53°$ **(1)**, $233°$ **(1)**

(c) (i) $\sin\theta = -\cos\theta \Rightarrow \dfrac{\sin\theta}{\cos\theta} = -1 \Rightarrow \tan\theta = -1$ **(1)**

(ii) $\tan(x - 10°) = -1$; $x - 10° = \tan^{-1}(-1)$;

$x - 10° = 135°, 315°$ **(2)**; $x = 145°, 325°$ **(2)**

SET 1 PAPER 2

1. Find critical values: $(x - 1)(x - 5) = 0$, $x = 1$, $x = 5$.

Test values near critical values: when $x = 0$, y is +ve,

when $x = 2$, y is −ve.

∴ $\geqslant 0$ when $x \leqslant 1$ and when $x \geqslant 5$. **(2)**

2. Multiplying through by x: $x^2 - 7x = 4 \Rightarrow x^2 - 7x - 4 = 0$. **(1)**

Quadratic formula with $a = 1$, $b = -7$, $c = -4$ to solve;

$x = \dfrac{7 \pm \sqrt{65}}{2}$ **(2)** or **(1)** if only one root.

3. $h = \dfrac{(1-0)}{5} = 0.2$ **(1)**

x	x^2	e^x	y
0	0	1.0	$y_0 = 0$
0.2	0.04	1.22140	$y_1 = 0.04886$
0.4	0.16	1.49182	$y_2 = 0.23869$
0.6	0.36	1.82212	$y_3 = 0.65596$
0.8	0.64	2.22554	$y_4 = 1.42435$ **(2 for all correct y values)**
1.0	1.0	2.71828	$y_5 = 2.71828$ **(1 for 4 values correct)**

$\frac{1}{2} \times 0.2 \times [0 + 2(0.04886 + 0.23869 + 0.65596 + 1.42435) +$

$2.71828]$ **(1)** $= 0.1 \times 7.4540 \approx 0.745$ to 3 s.f. **(1)**

4. (a) $x = \dfrac{1}{1+t} \Rightarrow t = \dfrac{1}{x} - 1;$ **(1)**

sub t into $y = t^2 + 4 \Rightarrow y = \left(\dfrac{1}{x} - 1\right)^2 + 4$

$\Rightarrow y = \dfrac{1}{x^2} - \dfrac{2}{x} + 5$ **(1)**

(b) $\dfrac{dx}{dt} = \dfrac{-1}{(1+t)^2}; \dfrac{dy}{dt} = 2t$ **(1)**; using chain rule,

$\dfrac{dy}{dt} \times \dfrac{dt}{dx} = 2t \times -1(1+t)^2$ **(1)** $\dfrac{dy}{dx} = -2t(1+t)^2$ **(1)**

When $t = 3$, $\dfrac{dy}{dx} = -6(4)^2 = -96$ **(1)**

5. LHS $= \cot^2\theta(\cot^2\theta + 1) \Rightarrow (\csc^2\theta - 1)(\csc^2\theta)$ **(1)**

[using $\csc^2\theta = 1 + \cot^2\theta$] **(1)**

$\Rightarrow \csc^4\theta - \csc^2\theta$, as required. **(1)**

6. (a) $u = \ln x, \dfrac{du}{dx} = \dfrac{1}{x}; \dfrac{dv}{dx} = x, v = \dfrac{1}{2}x^2$ **(1)**

$\ln x \times \dfrac{1}{2}x^2 - \int \dfrac{1}{2}x^2 \times \dfrac{1}{x} dx$ **(1)** $\Rightarrow \dfrac{1}{2}x^2 \ln x - \dfrac{1}{2}\int x\, dx$ **(1)**

$\dfrac{1}{2}x^2 \ln x - \dfrac{1}{4}x^2 + c$ **(2, 1 if +c omitted)**

(b) $\left[\dfrac{1}{2}x^2 \ln x - \dfrac{1}{4}x^2\right]$ with limits 0, 4 **(1)**

$\Rightarrow \left[\left(\dfrac{4^2 \ln 4}{2} - \dfrac{4^2}{4}\right) - \left(\dfrac{0^2 \ln 0}{2} - \dfrac{0^2}{4}\right)\right]$ **(1)** $= 8\ln 4 - 4$ **(1)**

7. $\displaystyle\lim_{h \to 0}\left[\dfrac{5(x+h)^3 - 8(x+h) + 4 - (5x^3 - 8x + 4)}{h}\right]$ **(2)**

$\Rightarrow \displaystyle\lim_{h \to 0}\left[15x^2 + 15xh + 5h^2 - 8\right]$ **(2)** so $\dfrac{dy}{dx} = 15x^2 - 8$ **(2)**

8. Suppose there's an odd number x for which x^2 is even **(1)**;

Since x is odd, $x = 2n - 1$, for some integer n. **(1)**

Then $x^2 = (2n-1)^2 = 4n^2 - 4n + 1$, which is odd since $4n^2$ and

$4n$ are both even. **(1)** $\therefore x^2$ can't be even. **(1)** $\therefore$ if x^2 is even,

x must also be even. **(1)**

9. (a) $\displaystyle\int \dfrac{1}{y+1}\, dy = \int 3x^2\, dx; \ln|y+1| = \dfrac{3x^3}{3} + c$ **(1)**;

$|y+1| = e^{x^3 + c}$ **(1)**; $|y+1| = e^{x^3} \times e^c$ **(1)**

$e^c = A$, so $|y+1| = Ae^{x^3}$ **(1)**. $\therefore y = Ae^{x^3} - 1$ is the general solution. **(1)**

(b) When $x = 0$ and $y = 5$, $5 = Ae^0 - 1$ so $A = 6$. **(1)**

Particular solution is $y = 6e^{x^3} - 1$ **(1)**

10. (a) (i) $|\mathbf{a}| = \sqrt{9^2 + (-2)^2 + (-6)^2} = 11$ **(1)**

(ii) $|\mathbf{b}| = \sqrt{2^2 + (-6)^2 + 3^2} = 7$ **(1)**

(iii) $|\overline{AB}| = \sqrt{(2-9)^2 + (-6+2)^2 + (3+6)^2} = \sqrt{146}$ **(2)**

(b) Using cosine rule **(1)**, $\left(\sqrt{146}\right)^2 = 11^2 + 7^2 - 2 \times 11 \times 7 \times \cos A$ **(1)**;

$\cos A = \dfrac{146 - 11^2 - 7^2}{-2 \times 11 \times 7}; \cos A = \dfrac{-24}{-154};$

$A = 81°$ **(1)**

11. $u_n = a + (n-1)d; u_{12} = 9 + (12-1) \times 7$ **(1)** $\Rightarrow u_{12} = 9 + 77 = 86$ **(1)**

12. Using rule $\displaystyle\int \dfrac{f'(x)}{f(x)} dx = \ln|f(x)| + c$ **(1)**

$f'(x) = 6x \Rightarrow \dfrac{1}{2}\int \dfrac{6x}{3x^2 + 1} dx$ **(1)** for $\dfrac{1}{2}$ **(1)** for correct numerator.

$= \dfrac{1}{2}\ln|3x^2 + 1| + c$ **(1)**

13. (a) Taking natural logs of both sides, $\ln e^x = \ln 7$; using the rule $\ln e^c = c$, $x = \ln 7$; $x = 1.95$ or better. **(1)**

(b) Taking natural logs of both sides, $\ln 3^x = \ln 20$;

$x\ln 3 = \ln 20$ **(1)**; $x = \dfrac{\ln 20}{\ln 3}$; $x = 2.73$ or better. **(1)**

14. (a) $\dfrac{d}{dx}x^2 + \dfrac{d}{dy}y^3 - \dfrac{d}{dx}4xy = \dfrac{d}{dx}(-14)$ **(1)**

$\Rightarrow 2x + \dfrac{d}{dx}y^3 - \dfrac{d}{dx}4xy = 0$ **(1)**

$\Rightarrow * \ 2x + 3y^2\dfrac{dy}{dx} - \dfrac{d}{dx}4xy = 0$ **(1)**;

$\dfrac{d}{dx}4xy$: Product rule: $u = 4x, \dfrac{du}{dx} = 4, v = y, \dfrac{dv}{dx} = \dfrac{dy}{dx},$

$\therefore \dfrac{d}{dx}4xy = 4x\dfrac{dy}{dx} + 4y$ **(1)**. Sub this back into *.

$\Rightarrow 2x + 3y^2\dfrac{dy}{dx} - \left(4x\dfrac{dy}{dx} + 4y\right) = 0$ **(1)**;

$\dfrac{dy}{dx}(3y^2 - 4x) = 4y - 2x; \dfrac{dy}{dx} = \dfrac{4y - 2x}{3y^2 - 4x}$ **(1)**

(b) For gradient at (1, 2), sub $x = 1$ and $y = 2$ into the answer to **(a)**. Gradient $= \dfrac{3}{4}$ **(1)**

15. Make y the subject of the 1st equation: $y = \dfrac{(2x-1)}{2}$ **(1)**.

Sub this for y in the 2nd equation:

$x^2 - x\left(\dfrac{2x-1}{2}\right) + 2\left(\dfrac{2x-1}{2}\right)^2 = 8$ **(1)**

$x^2 - \left(\dfrac{2x^2 - x}{2}\right) + \left(\dfrac{8x^2 - 8x + 2}{4}\right) = 8 \Rightarrow 8x^2 - 6x - 30 = 30$ **(1)**.

Quadratic equation to solve: $x = 2.3474, x = -1.597$ **(1)**. Sub each of this into expression for y to get $y = 1.8474, y = -2.097$. **(1)**

Solutions are (2.35, 1.85), (–1.60, –2.10) or better **(2)**

16. $\cos 75° = \cos(45° + 30°)$ **(1)**; using addition formulae,

$\cos(45° + 30°) = \cos 45° \cos 30° - \sin 45° \sin 30°$ **(1)**;

$\cos(45° + 30°) = \left(\dfrac{1}{\sqrt{2}} \times \dfrac{\sqrt{3}}{2}\right) - \left(\dfrac{1}{\sqrt{2}} \times \dfrac{1}{2}\right)$ **(1)**

$\Rightarrow \dfrac{1}{2\sqrt{2}}\left(\sqrt{3} - 1\right)$ **(1)** $= \dfrac{\sqrt{2}}{4}\left(\sqrt{3} - 1\right)$ **(1)**

17. $\int_0^4 e^{2x}\, dx = \left[\dfrac{e^{2x}}{2}\right]$ **(1)** with limits 0 and 4 **(1)**.

$\left[\dfrac{e^8}{2} - \dfrac{e^0}{2}\right] = \dfrac{1}{2}(e^8 - 1)$ **(2, 1 if not in exact form)**

18. LHS $= \dfrac{\sin\theta}{\cos\theta} + \dfrac{\cos\theta}{\sin\theta} \Rightarrow \dfrac{\sin^2\theta + \cos^2\theta}{\cos\theta\sin\theta}$ **(1)** $\Rightarrow \dfrac{1}{\cos\theta\sin\theta}$

(using identity $\sin^2\theta + \cos^2\theta \equiv 1$) **(1)**

$\Rightarrow \dfrac{2}{2\cos\theta\sin\theta}$ **(1)** $\Rightarrow \dfrac{2}{\sin 2\theta}$ (using double angle identity) **(1)**

$\Rightarrow 2\mathrm{cosec}\, 2\theta = $ RHS as required **(2)**

19. $\int 12x(3x - 0.5)^{\frac{1}{2}}\, dx = \int 1 \ dt$ **(1)**

Using integration by parts **(1)**

$u = 12x,\ \dfrac{du}{dx} = 12$ **(1)** $\dfrac{dv}{dx} = (3x - 0.5)^{\frac{1}{2}};\ v = \int (3x - 0.5)^{\frac{1}{2}}\, dx$

Use integration by substitution to find v, using $u = 3x - 0.5$ **(1)**

$\Rightarrow v = \dfrac{2}{9}(3x - 0.5)^{\frac{3}{2}}$ **(1)**

$12x \times \dfrac{2}{9}(3x - 0.5)^{\frac{3}{2}} - 12\int \dfrac{2}{9}(3x - 0.5)^{\frac{3}{2}}\, dx$ **(1)**

$\Rightarrow \dfrac{8x}{3}(3x - 0.5)^{\frac{3}{2}} - \dfrac{8}{3}\int (3x - 0.5)^{\frac{3}{2}}\, dx$ **(1)**

$\Rightarrow \dfrac{8x}{3}(3x - 0.5)^{\frac{3}{2}} - \dfrac{8}{3} \times \dfrac{1}{3} \times \dfrac{(3x - 0.5)^{\frac{5}{2}}}{\frac{5}{2}} + c$ **(1)**

$= \dfrac{8x}{3}(3x - 0.5)^{\frac{3}{2}} - \dfrac{16}{45}(3x - 0.5)^{\frac{5}{2}} + c$ **(1)**

Since $\int 1\ dt = t + c$, when $t = 0$, $x = 0.5$. Substituting these values into the equation above gives $c = -\dfrac{44}{45}$ **(1)**

$\therefore t = \dfrac{8x}{3}(3x - 0.5)^{\frac{3}{2}} - \dfrac{16}{45}(3x - 0.5)^{\frac{5}{2}} - \dfrac{44}{45}$ **(1)**

SET 1 PAPER 3 – SECTION A – STATISTICS

1. **(a)** $140 + 176 + 122 = 438$ **(1)**;
$A : \dfrac{140}{438} \times 100 = 31.96\% \approx 32\%$ **(1)**

(b) Office C = 27.85%; 27.85% of 40 = 11.14 ≈ 11 people **(1)**

2. **(a)** Fig 1: very little correlation between daily max gust in 1987 and 2015 **(1)**; outlier of about 66 in 1987, indicator of the great storm 1987 **(1)**

Fig 2: strong +ve correlation between windspeed and gust in 1987 **(1)**; outlier indicative of great storm in 1987 **(1)**

(b) P(R > 1 s.d. below mean); P = 0.15866 **(1)**,
31 × 0.15866 = 4.91 days **(1)**

3. **(a)**

	1987	2015
Hurn	17.06	17.39
Beijing	24.24	24.95
Camborne	15.12	16.44

(2 marks all correct, 1 for 4 or more correct values)

(b)

	1987	2015
Hurn	2.13	2.51
Beijing	1.46	2.02
Camborne	1.40	1.30

(2 marks all correct, 1 for 4 or more correct values)

(c) Although there is an increase in the mean for all 3 locations, it is a very short time period and so not enough data **(1)**. There is a small change in the standard deviations which could suggest extreme weather **(1)**.

There was in fact a heatwave in the UK at the end of June, beginning of July in 2015, which would explain the increase in the mean **(1)**.

(d) She did not consider enough places. **(1)**
She did not consider enough different months (to see if a pattern is repeated at different times of year) **(1)**

4. **(a)** $P(x = 7) = \dfrac{9 - 7}{16}$ **(1)** $= \dfrac{1}{8}$ **(1)**

(b) $P(x \le 6) = \dfrac{2 - 1}{16}$ **(1)** $+ \dfrac{3 - 1}{16} + \dfrac{4 - 1}{16} + \dfrac{5 - 1}{16}$ **(1)** $+ \dfrac{9 - 6}{16}$ **(1)**
$= \dfrac{13}{16}$ **(1)**

5. $H_0 : \mu = 26.4;\ H_1 : \mu \ne 26.4$ **(2)**

$X \sim N(26.4, 6.9^2);\ \alpha = 0.05,\ \dfrac{\alpha}{2} = 0.025$, giving $Z = \pm 1.96$ **(1)**;

$\bar{x} = 30.9,\ n = 14,\ \bar{X} \sim N(30.9, 8.14^2)$ **(1)**

Therefore, the test statistic is: $\dfrac{\bar{x} - \mu}{\frac{\sigma}{\sqrt{n}}} = \dfrac{30.9 - 26.4}{\frac{6.9}{\sqrt{14}}} = 2.44$ **(1)**

$P(Z \ge 2.44) = 1 - P(Z < 2.44)$
$= 1 - 0.99266 = 0.00734 < \dfrac{\alpha}{2}$ **(1)**

So H_0 is rejected in favour of H_1 **(1)**
There is significant evidence to suggest that a change in mean time taken to complete the puzzle has occurred. **(1)**

6. **(a)** $P(X > 25) \Rightarrow 1 - P\left(Z > \dfrac{25 - 19}{6}\right)$ **(1)** $\Rightarrow 1 - 0.84134$ **(1)**
$= 0.159$ **(1)**

(b) $P(X < 12) \Rightarrow P\left(Z > \dfrac{12 - 19}{6}\right)$ **(1)**
$= 0.122$ **(1)** or 12.2% **(1)**

(c) $P(16 < X < 22) = 0.383$ **(2)**

7. **(a)** $P(D \cap C \cap R) = 0.3 \times 0.4 \times 0.2 = 0.024$ **(1)**
(b) $P(D' \cap C' \cap R') = 0.7 \times 0.6 \times 0.8 = 0.0336$ **(1)**
(c) $P(D' \cap C' \cap R) = 0.7 \times 0.6 \times 0.2 = 0.084$ **(2)**
(d) $0.3 \times 0.6 \times 0.8 + 0.7 \times 0.4 \times 0.8 + 0.7 \times 0.6 \times 0.2 = 0.452$ **(3)**
(e) $P(D_A \cap D_E) = P(D_A | D_E) \times P(D_E) = 0.8 \times 0.3 = 0.24$ **(3)**

SET 1 PAPER 3 - SECTION B – MECHANICS

8. $F = ma \Rightarrow 8 = m \times 5 \Rightarrow m = \dfrac{8}{5} = 1.6$ kg **(1)**

9. **(a)** Resolving vertically, $T = 20 + 35 = 55$N **(1)**
(b) Taking moments about midpoint, $35s = 3 \times 20$ **(1)**; $s = \dfrac{60}{35}$;
$s = 1.71$ m **(1)**

10. **(a)** $0.5 \times 2.4 \times 27.8 + 0.5 \times (27.8 + 55.6) \times 2 + 0.5 \times (55.6 + 83.3) \times 4$ **(2)** $= 33.36 + 83.4 + 277.8$ **(1)** $= 394.56$ m **(1)**
(b) $\dfrac{394.56}{8.4} = 46.97$ m s^{-1} **(2)**

11. **(a)** $F_1 + F_2 + F_3 = (6 + 8 - 4)\mathbf{i} + (7 - 5 + 3)\mathbf{j}$ **(1)** $= 10\mathbf{i} + 5\mathbf{j}$ **(1)**
(b) $|10\mathbf{i} + 5\mathbf{j}| = \sqrt{10^2 + 5^2} = \sqrt{125} = 5\sqrt{5}$ **(2)**

(c) $m = 4\text{kg}$, $F = 5\sqrt{5}$ N. Using $F = ma$, $5\sqrt{5} = 4a$,

$a = \dfrac{5\sqrt{5}}{4}$, $a = 2.795$ m s^{-2} **(2)**

(d) $\tan\theta = \dfrac{5}{10}$ **(1)**; $\theta = \tan^{-1}\left(\dfrac{5}{10}\right)$; $\theta = 26.6°$ **(1)**

12. (a) $31\sin\theta - 3 \times 9.8 = 0$ **(1)**; $\sin\theta = \dfrac{(3 \times 9.8)}{31}$ **(1)**;

∴ $\sin\theta = 0.948$ as required **(1)**

(b) Using $s = ut + \dfrac{1}{2}at^2$, $h_{max} = 31 \times \sin\theta \times 3 - \dfrac{1}{2} \times 9.8 \times 3^2$ **(1)**;

$h_{max} = 44.064$ **(1)**, or 44.1 to 3 s. f. **(1)**

(c) $\sin\theta = \dfrac{(3 \times 9.8)}{31}$ (from (a)) **(1)**, $\theta = 71.44°$ **(1)**;

PR $= 31 \times 0.318 \times 6 = 59.1$ m **(1)**

13. (a) Using $F = ma$, $T - 900 = 1500 \times 0.5$ **(1)**; $T = 750 + 900$ **(1)**;

$T = 1650$ N **(1)**

(b) $3200 - 900 - F = 4500 \times 0.5$ **(2)**; $F = 2300 - 2250$ **(1)**;

$F = 50$ N **(1)**

14. (a) $s = 2(6)^3 - 5(6)^2 + 3(6)$; $s = 270$ m at $t = 6$ **(1)**

(b) $v = \dfrac{ds}{dt}$; $\dfrac{ds}{dt} = 6t^2 - 10t + 3$ **(1)**; at $t = 2$,

$\dfrac{ds}{dt} = 6(2)^2 - 10(2) + 3$; $v = 7$ m s^{-1} **(1)**

15. $v = \dfrac{dr}{dt} = \left[\dfrac{d}{dt}(t^2 + 3)\right]\mathbf{i} + \left[\dfrac{d}{dt}(3t - 4)\right]\mathbf{j} = 2t\mathbf{i} + 3\mathbf{j}$ m s^{-1} **(2)**

sub $t = 4$ into the equation: $v = 2 \times 4\mathbf{i} + 3\mathbf{j} = 8\mathbf{i} + 3\mathbf{j}$ m s^{-1} **(2)**

Using Pythagoras to find speed, $\sqrt{8^2 + 3^2} = 8.54$ m s^{-1} **(1)**.

$\tan\theta = \dfrac{3}{8}$ **(1)**; $\theta = 20.6°$ from the $\mathbf{i}$-direction. **(1)**

16. (a) (1) for correct diagram

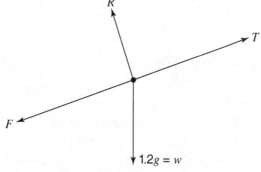

1.2$g = w$

(b) $R = 1.2g \cos34°$ **(2)**; $R = 9.75$N **(1)**

(c) Using $F_{max} = \mu R$, $F = 0.28 \times 9.75$ **(1)**, $F = 2.73$N **(1)**

EDEXCEL SET 2 PAPER 1

1. $5 \times 2\theta\left(1 - \dfrac{1}{2}(2\theta)^2\right) = 10\theta\left(1 - 2\theta^2\right) = 10\theta - 20\theta^3$ **(2)**

2. (a) $x^2 - 6x + y^2 + 2y - 15 = 0$

$\Rightarrow (x - 3)^2 - 9(y + 1)^2 - 1 - 15 = 0$ **(1)**

$\Rightarrow (x - 3)^2 + (y + 1)^2 = 25$ **(1)**.

Centre $(3, -1)$, radius $\sqrt{25} = 5$. **(1)**

(b) (i) Differentiating (implicitly) wrt x,

$2x + 2y\dfrac{dy}{dx} - 6 + 2\dfrac{dy}{dx} = 0$ **(1)**;

$\dfrac{dy}{dx}(2y + 2) = 6 - 2x$ **(1)**;

$\dfrac{dy}{dx} = \dfrac{6 - 2x}{2y + 2}$ **(1)**; $\dfrac{dy}{dx} = \dfrac{6 - 2(7)}{2(2) + 2}$ **(1)**; $\dfrac{dy}{dx} = \dfrac{-4}{3}$ **(1)**;

Using $y - y_1 = m(x - x_1)$, $y - 2 = \dfrac{-4}{3}(x - 7)$ **(1)**;

$3y - 6 = -4x + 28$ **(1)**; $3y + 4x = 34$ **(1)**

(ii) Gradient of normal is (–ve) reciprocal. $\dfrac{dy}{dx} = \dfrac{3}{4}$ **(1)**;

$y - 2 = \dfrac{3}{4}(x - 7) \Rightarrow 4y - 8 = 3x - 21$ **(1)**

$\Rightarrow 4y - 3x = -13$

3. (a)

x	$x + 1$	$y = \sqrt{x + 1}$
0	1	$y_0 = 1$
0.25	1.25	$y_1 = \sqrt{\dfrac{5}{2}} = 1.118034$
0.5	1.5	$y_2 = \sqrt{\dfrac{6}{2}} = 1.224745$
0.75	1.75	$y_3 = \sqrt{\dfrac{7}{2}} = 1.322876$
1.0	2	$y_4 = \sqrt{2} = 1.414214$ **(2)**

$\dfrac{1}{2} \times \dfrac{1}{4}\left[\left(1 + \sqrt{2}\right) + 2\left(\sqrt{\dfrac{5}{2}} + \sqrt{\dfrac{6}{2}} + \sqrt{\dfrac{7}{2}}\right)\right]$ **(1)** $= 1.218$ to 4 s.f. **(1)**

(b) increase the number of strips. **(1)**

4. (a) $\dfrac{\sqrt{25} \times \sqrt{2}}{5} = \dfrac{5\sqrt{2}}{5} = \sqrt{2}$ **(1)**

(b) $7\sqrt{2} - \sqrt{36}\sqrt{2} = 7\sqrt{2} - 6\sqrt{2} = \sqrt{2}$ **(1)**

(c) $\dfrac{\sqrt{22}}{\sqrt{11}} = \dfrac{\sqrt{2}\sqrt{11}}{\sqrt{11}} = \sqrt{2}$ **(1)**

∴ All answers are equal, as required.

5. (a) $y = 2\cos x$ **(1)** for correct shape **(1)** for correct intercepts.

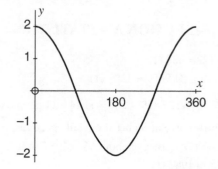

(b) $y = \cos2x$ **(1)** for correct shape **(1)** for correct intercepts.

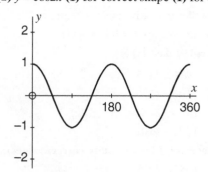

(c) $y = \cos(x + 30°)$ **(1)** for correct shape **(1)** for correct intercepts.

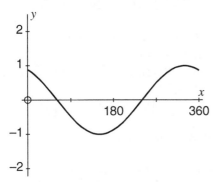

Each part: **(2)** fully correct or **(1)** for correct shape

6. (a) $f(1) = 1^3 + 3 \times 1^2 - 1 - 3 = 0$ **(1)**

(b) $(x - 1)(x^2 + ax + b)$ **(1)** $\Rightarrow ax^3 + ax^2 + bx - x^2 - ax - b$.
Comparing coefficients gives $a = 4$ **(1)**, $b = 1$ **(1)**;
$x^2 + 4x + 3 = (x + 1)(x + 3)$
$x^3 + 3x^2 - x - 3 = (x - 1)(x + 1)(x + 3)$ **(1)**

7. (a) Quotient rule: $u = x + 4$, $\dfrac{du}{dx} = 1$ **(1)**,

$v = 1 + x^2$, $\dfrac{dv}{dx} = 2x$ **(1)**; $\dfrac{1(1 + x^2) - 2x(x + 4)}{(1 + x^2)^2}$ **(1)**

$= \dfrac{-x^2 - 8x + 1}{(1 + x^2)^2}$ **(1)**

(b) At stationary point, $\dfrac{dy}{dx} = 0$. $\dfrac{-x^2 - 8x + 1}{(1 + x^2)^2} = 0$ **(1)**

$\Rightarrow -x^2 - 8x + 1 = 0$;
Quadratic formula gives $x = -4 \pm \sqrt{17}$ **(2)**

8. (2 for correct shape, 1 for correct x-intercepts)

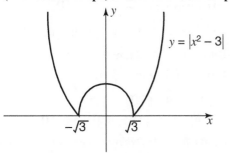

$y = |x^2 - 3|$

9. Expanding LHS gives $\sin^2\theta + 2\sin\theta\,\text{cosec}\,\theta + \text{cosec}^2\,\theta$ **(1)**;

$\sin^2\theta + \dfrac{2\sin\theta}{\sin\theta} + 1 + \cot^2\theta$ (using $\text{cosec}^2\theta = 1 + \cot^2\theta$) **(1)**;

$\sin^2\theta + \cot^2\theta + 3$ as required. **(1)**

10. $u = 3x + 1$, $\dfrac{du}{dx} = 3$, $dx = \dfrac{du}{3}$, $x = \dfrac{u - 1}{3}$ **(1)**;

$\int\left(\dfrac{u - 1}{3}\right)u^6 \dfrac{du}{3} \Rightarrow \dfrac{1}{9}\int(u - 1)u^6\,du \Rightarrow \dfrac{1}{9}\int u^7 - u^6\,du$ **(1)**,

$\dfrac{1}{9} \times \left(\dfrac{u^8}{8} - \dfrac{u^7}{7}\right) + c$ **(1)**

$\Rightarrow \dfrac{1}{9} \times \left(\dfrac{(3x + 1)^8}{8} - \dfrac{(3x + 1)^7}{7}\right) + c$ **(1)**

11. $\log_a x = \log_a 4^3 - \log_a 2^3$ **(1)** $\Rightarrow \log_a 64 - \log_a 8$ **(1)**

$= \log_a \dfrac{64}{8} = \log_a 8$; $\log_a x = \log_a 8$, $\therefore x = 8$ **(1)**

12. $a = 4$, $u_9 = 4 + 8d$ **(1)**, $u_2 = 4 + d$ **(1)**;
$u_9 = 4u_2 \Rightarrow 4 + 8d = 4(4 + d)$ **(1)**.

$S_{10} = \dfrac{10}{2}(2 \times 4 + (10 - 1) \times 3$ **(1)** $\Rightarrow S_{10} = 5(8 + 27) = 175$ **(1)**

13. (a) Using $\dfrac{1}{2}ab\sin C$, $\dfrac{1}{2} \times 6 \times 6 \times \sin\theta = 17.6$ **(1)**;

$\sin\theta = \dfrac{17.6}{18}$; $\theta = 1.35958^c$ **(1)**

(b) $\dfrac{1}{2}r^2\theta = \dfrac{1}{2} \times 6^2 \times 1.35958^c$ **(1)** $= 24.472$ cm² **(1)**

(c) $24.472 - 17.6 = 6.87$ cm² or better **(1)**

14. (a) (i) $f(x) \geq 1$ **(1)**;

(ii) $g(x) \geq 0$ **(1)**;

(iii) $fg(x) = 3(2x^2) + 1 \Rightarrow fg(x) = 6x^2 + 1$ **(1)**; $fg(x) \geq 1$ **(1)**

(b) (i) $y = \dfrac{1}{2x - 6}$; swap x and y: $x = \dfrac{1}{2y - 6}$ **(1)**:

Rearrange to make y the subject:
$2y - 6 = \dfrac{1}{x} \Rightarrow 2y = \dfrac{1}{x} + 6 \Rightarrow 2y = \dfrac{1 + 6x}{x}$ **(1)**

$\Rightarrow y = \dfrac{1 + 6x}{2x}$ **(1)** $\left(\text{or } y = \dfrac{1}{2x} + 3\right)$

(ii) $x \in R, x \neq 0$ **(1)**

15. (a) Use the rule $\int \dfrac{f'(x)}{f(x)}\,dx = \ln|f(x)| + c$ **(1)**

$\Rightarrow \ln|\sin x| + c$ **(1)**

(b) Same rule as (a): $\dfrac{d}{dx}4x^2 + 3 = 8x$ **(1)**; $\dfrac{1}{2}\int \dfrac{4x}{4x^2 + 3}\,dx$ **(1)**

$= \dfrac{1}{2}\ln|4x^2 + 3| + c$ **(1)**

16. (a) $\int 1\,dy = \int \dfrac{x}{x^2 + 1}\,dx$ **(1)**; $y = \dfrac{1}{2}\int \dfrac{2x}{x^2 + 1}\,dx$ **(1)**

$= \dfrac{1}{2}\ln|x^2 + 1| + c$ **(1)**

(b) $2 = \dfrac{1}{2}\ln|3^2 + 1| + c$; $2 = \dfrac{1}{2}\ln 10 + c \Rightarrow c = 2 - \dfrac{1}{2}\ln 10$ **(1)**;

$y = \dfrac{1}{2}\ln|x^2 + 1| - \dfrac{1}{2}\ln 10 + 2$; $y = \dfrac{1}{2}\ln\left(\dfrac{x^2 + 1}{10}\right) + 2$ **(1)**

17. (a) $R\cos(x + a) = R(\cos x \cos\alpha - \sin x \sin\alpha)$;
$5\cos x - 3\sin x \equiv R\cos x \cos\alpha - R\sin x \sin\alpha$ **(1)**;
$5\cos x = R\cos x \cos\alpha$, $*5 = R\cos\alpha$, $-3\sin x = -R\sin x \sin\alpha$,
$**3 = R\sin\alpha$ **(1)** $\tan x = \dfrac{R\sin\alpha}{R\cos\alpha} = \dfrac{3}{5}$, $x = 31°$ **(1)**;

Squaring both expressions * and **, and adding them,
gives $R^2\cos^2\alpha + R^2\sin^2\alpha = 25 + 9$;
$R^2(\cos^2\alpha + \sin^2\alpha) = 34$ **(1)**
$R = \sqrt{34}$, so $5\cos x - 3\sin x \equiv \sqrt{34}\cos(x + 31°)$ **(1)**

(b) $\sqrt{34}\cos(x + 31°) = 2 \Rightarrow \cos(x + 31°) = \dfrac{2}{\sqrt{34}}$ **(1)**;

$x + 31° = \cos^{-1}\left(\dfrac{2}{\sqrt{34}}\right) = 69.9°$, $360° - 69.9° = 290.1°$ **(1)**;

$x = 69.9° - 31° = 38.9°$ **(1)**, $x = 290.1° - 31° = 259.1°$ **(1)**

18. (a) $p = 7$, $2p + 1 = 15$ which is not prime. **(2)**

(b) $a = \sqrt{2}$, $b = \sqrt{2}$, $ab = 2$ which is not irrational **(2)**

19. $\left(1 + \dfrac{x}{2}\right)^4 = 1 + \begin{pmatrix} 4 \\ 1 \end{pmatrix}\dfrac{x}{2} + \begin{pmatrix} 4 \\ 2 \end{pmatrix}\left(\dfrac{x}{2}\right)^2 + \begin{pmatrix} 4 \\ 3 \end{pmatrix}\left(\dfrac{x}{2}\right)^3$ **(2)**

$\Rightarrow 1 + 2x + \dfrac{6x^2}{4} + \dfrac{4x^3}{8}$ **(1)** $\Rightarrow 1 + 2x + \dfrac{3x^2}{2} + \dfrac{x^3}{2}$

$\therefore a = 2, b = 1.5, c = 0.5$ **(1)** (allow $1 + 2x \ldots$)

EDEXCEL SET 2 PAPER 2

1. $6 - 6x \geqslant 4x + 8; \ -10x \geqslant 2; \ -x \geqslant \dfrac{1}{5}; x \leqslant -\dfrac{1}{5}$ **(1)**

2. $\dfrac{dy}{dx} = 3(-5e^{3x-1})$ **(1)** $\Rightarrow \dfrac{dy}{dx} = -15e^{3x-1}$ **(1)**

3. $7^2 = 4^2 + 5^2 - 2 \times 4 \times 5 \times \cos A \Rightarrow \cos A = \dfrac{49-41}{-40};$

$A = 101.5°$ **(1)**

4. **(a)** sub $y = x + 1$ into equation for circle, then expand.

$x^2 + (x - 1)^2 = 25$ **(1)**; $2x^2 - 2x - 24 = 0$ **(1)**;

Divide by 2: $x^2 - x - 12 = 0$ **(1)**

(b) $(x - 4)(x + 3) = 0$ **(1)**; $x = 4, x = -3, M = (4, 3),$

$N = (-3, -4)$ **(2)**

5. $\dfrac{dx}{dt} = 6t + 4$ **(1)**, $\dfrac{dy}{dt} = 3t^2 + 2t$ **(1)**; Chain rule:

$\dfrac{dy}{dx} = \dfrac{dy}{dt} \times \dfrac{dt}{dx} \Rightarrow \dfrac{3t^2 + 2t}{6t + 4} \times \dfrac{t(3t + 2)}{2(3t + 2)}$ **(1)** $= \dfrac{t}{2}$ **(1)**

6. $\sin^2 x = \dfrac{1}{2}(1 - \cos 2x)$ **(1)**,

$\therefore \displaystyle\int_{-\frac{\pi}{4}}^{\frac{\pi}{4}} \dfrac{\sin^2 x}{3} \, dx = \dfrac{1}{6}\displaystyle\int_{-\frac{\pi}{4}}^{\frac{\pi}{4}} 1 - \cos 2x \, dx$ **(1)**

$= \dfrac{1}{6}\left[x - \dfrac{\sin 2x}{2}\right]_{-\frac{\pi}{4}}^{\frac{\pi}{4}}$ **(1)**

$= \dfrac{1}{6}\left[\left(\dfrac{\pi}{4} - \dfrac{1}{2}\sin\left(\dfrac{\pi}{2}\right)\right) - \left(-\dfrac{\pi}{4} - \dfrac{1}{2}\sin\left(-\dfrac{\pi}{2}\right)\right)\right]$ **(1)**

$= \dfrac{1}{6}\left[\dfrac{\pi}{4} - \dfrac{1}{2} + \dfrac{\pi}{4} - \dfrac{1}{2}\right]$ **(1)** $= \dfrac{1}{6}\left[\dfrac{\pi}{2} - 1\right] = \dfrac{\pi}{12} - \dfrac{1}{6}$ **(1)**

7. **(a)** $a = \dfrac{1}{2}$ **(1)**, $r = -\dfrac{1}{2}$ **(1)**; $\dfrac{\frac{1}{2}}{1 - \left(-\frac{1}{2}\right)} = \dfrac{\frac{1}{2}}{\frac{3}{2}} = \dfrac{1}{3}$ **(2)**

(b) $S_\infty = \dfrac{a}{1 - r} = 6; \dfrac{5}{1 - r} = 6$ **(1)**; $\dfrac{5}{6} = 1 - r$ **(1)**;

$r = 1 - \dfrac{5}{6} = \dfrac{1}{6}$ **(1)**

8. **(a)** $\dfrac{dT}{dt} = -kT$ **(2)**

(b) $\displaystyle\int \dfrac{1}{T} \, dT = -k\displaystyle\int 1 \, dt$ **(1)** $\Rightarrow \ln T = -kt + c$ **(1)** $e^{\ln T} = e^{-kt+c}$ **(1)**

$\Rightarrow T = e^c \times e^{-kt}$ **(1)**

(c) At $t = 0, T = 74 - 16 = 58, \therefore e^c = 58$ **(1)**; at $t = 5,$

$T = 62 - 16 = 46$ **(1)**; $46 = 58e^{-5k}; e^{-5k} = \dfrac{46}{58} = \dfrac{23}{39}$ **(1)**

At $t = 10; T = 58e^{-10k}$ **(1)**

$\Rightarrow 58\left(e^{-5k}\right)^2 \Rightarrow 58\left(\dfrac{23}{39}\right)^2 = 36.5°C$ **(1):**

$36.5°C + 16 = 52.5°C$ **(1)**

9. **(a)** $f(0) = e^{2 \times 0} + 4(0) - 5 = -4; f(1) = e^{2 \times 1} + 4(1) - 5 = 6.389$ **(1)**

Change of sign, $\therefore$ a root lies in this interval **(1)**.

(b) $f'(x) = 2e^{2x} + 4; f(0.5) = -0.281718$ **(1)**, $f'(0.5) = 9.43656$ **(1)**;

$x_2 = 0.5 - \dfrac{-0.281718}{9.43656}$ **(1)** $= 0.52985$ **(1)**

10. **(a)** $\mathbf{m}_{new} = (3\mathbf{i} - 4\mathbf{j}) + (3\mathbf{i} + 6\mathbf{j}) = (6\mathbf{i} + 2\mathbf{j})$ **(1)**;

$\mathbf{n}_{new} = (6\mathbf{i} + 2\mathbf{j}) \times 2 = 12\mathbf{i} + 4\mathbf{j}$ **(1)**;

$\mathbf{n}_{new} - \mathbf{m}_{new} = (6\mathbf{i} + 2\mathbf{j})$ **(1)**; $\sqrt{6^2 + 2^2} = \sqrt{40} = 2\sqrt{10}$ **(1)**

(b) $\overrightarrow{MN} = \mathbf{n} - \mathbf{m} = \begin{pmatrix} 6 \\ 2 \end{pmatrix}$ **(1)**; $\overrightarrow{NP} = \mathbf{p} - \mathbf{n} = \begin{pmatrix} 3 \\ 1 \end{pmatrix}$ **(1)**;

$\overrightarrow{MN} = 2\overrightarrow{NP} \ \therefore$ collinear **(1)**

11. **(a)** $\left(1 - \dfrac{1}{2}\theta^2\right) + 3\theta = 1 + 3\theta - \dfrac{1}{2}\theta^2$ **(1)**

(b) $\dfrac{3\tan\theta - \theta}{\sin 2\theta} = \dfrac{3\theta - \theta}{2\theta} = 1$ **(2)**

(c) $\dfrac{1 - \cos\theta}{\tan\theta} = \dfrac{1 - \left(1 - \frac{1}{2}\theta^2\right)}{\theta} = \dfrac{\frac{1}{2}\theta^2}{\theta} = \dfrac{1}{2}\theta$ **(3)**

(d) $\dfrac{\sqrt{3} - \sin\theta}{\cos\theta} = \dfrac{\sqrt{3} - \theta}{1 - \frac{1}{2}\theta^2} = \dfrac{2\sqrt{3} - 2\theta}{2 - \theta^2} = \dfrac{2(\sqrt{3} - \theta)}{2 - \theta^2}$ **(3)**

12. **(a)** $3 \equiv A(x - 1) + B(2x + 1)$ **(1)**; $B = 1, A = -2$ **(1)**

$\Rightarrow \dfrac{3}{(2x + 1)(x - 1)} = \dfrac{-2}{(2x + 1)} + \dfrac{1}{(x - 1)}$ **(1)**

(b) $\displaystyle\int_2^3 \dfrac{-2}{2x + 1} + \dfrac{1}{x - 1} \, dx = \left[-\ln |2x + 1| + \ln |x - 1|\right]$ **(1)**

$\Rightarrow [(-\ln 7 + \ln 2) - (-\ln 5 + \ln 1)]$ **(1)**

$\Rightarrow \ln\dfrac{1}{7} + \ln 2 + \ln 5$ **(1)** $\Rightarrow \ln\dfrac{2}{7} + \ln 5 = \ln\dfrac{10}{7}$ **(1)**

13. $\dfrac{dy}{dx} = 3x^2 + 12x + 12$ **(1)**; divide by 3: $x^2 + 4x + 4 = 0;$

$(x + 2)^2 = 0$ **(1)**, $x = -2$ **(1)**; $y = -8 + 24 - 24 + 12 = 4$ **(1)**;

$\dfrac{d^2y}{dx^2} = 6x + 12$ **(1)**, When $x = -2, \dfrac{d^2y}{dx^2} = 0$ **(1)**,

$\therefore$ one stationary point at $(-2, 4)$, point of inflection **(1)**

14. $2(1 + \tan^2\theta) - 3 + \tan\theta = 0$ **(1)**; $2\tan^2\theta + \tan\theta - 1 = 0$ **(1)**;

Factorising, $\tan\theta = \dfrac{1}{2}$ **(1)**, $\tan\theta = -1$ **(1)**;

$\theta = 26.6°, 26.6° + 180° = 206.6°$ **(1)**;

$\theta = -45°, -45° + 180° = 135°, 135° + 180° = 315°$ **(1)**

15. Let the 3-digit number be abc, where a is hundreds, b is tens, c is units **(1)**. $abc = 100a + 10b + c$ **(1)**;

$100a + 10b + c = 99a + 9b + (a + b + c)$ **(1)**; Let $a + b + c = 3d,$ for some number d **(1)**; $100a + 10b + c = 99a + 9b + 3d$ **(1)**;

$100a + 10b + c = 3(33a + 3b + d)$ **(1)**;

$\therefore abc$ can be written as a multiple of 3. **(1)**

16. **(a)** $f'(x) = \displaystyle\lim_{h \to 0}\left[\dfrac{\left(4(x + h)^2 - 5(x + h) + 2\right) - (4x^2 - 5x + 2)}{h}\right]$ **(1)**

$= \displaystyle\lim_{h \to 0}\left[\dfrac{\left(4\left(x^2 + 2xh + h^2\right) - 5x - 5h + 2\right) - (4x^2 - 5x + 2)}{h}\right]$ **(2)**

$= \displaystyle\lim_{h \to 0}\left[\dfrac{8xh + 4h^2 - 5h}{h}\right]$ **(2)**

$= 8x + 4h - 5$ **(1)**; as $h \to 0, f'(x) = 8x - 5$ **(1)**

(b) $\dfrac{dy}{dx} = 8x - 5; 8x - 5 > 0$ **(1)**, $8x > 5, x > \dfrac{5}{8}$ **(1)**

17. (a) Chain rule. $y = \cos u$, $\dfrac{dy}{du} = -\sin u$; $u = 6x - 5$, $\dfrac{du}{dx} = 6$ **(1)**;

$\dfrac{dy}{dx} = \dfrac{dy}{du} \times \dfrac{du}{dx} = -6\sin(6x - 5)$ **(1)**

(b) Chain rule.

$y = \ln u$, $\dfrac{dy}{du} = \dfrac{1}{u}$; $u = x^3 - 5x + 1$, $\dfrac{du}{dx} = 3x^2 - 5$ **(1)**.

$\dfrac{dy}{dx} = \dfrac{dy}{du} \times \dfrac{du}{dx} = \dfrac{3x^2 - 5}{x^3 - 5x + 1}$ **(1)**

EDEXCEL SET 2 PAPER 3 – SECTION A - STATISTICS

1. (a) (i) $0.25 \times 0.15 \times 0.2 = 0.0075$ **(2)**

   (ii) $0.65 \times 0.6 \times 0.75 = 0.2925$ **(2)**

   (iii) P (2 choose green) $= 0.1 \times 0.45 \times 0.45 + 0.1 \times 0.55$
   $\times 0.55 + 0.9 \times 0.45 \times 0.55 = 0.27325$ **(2)**

   P (all 3 choose green) $= 0.1 \times 0.45 \times 0.55$
   $= 0.02475$ **(1)**

   P (2 or more) $=$ P(2) + P(all 3) $= 0.27325 + 0.02475$
   $= 0.298$ **(1)**

   (b) (i) P(GG) $= 0.25 \times 0.8 = 0.2$ **(1)**;

   P(SS) $= 0.55 \times 0.6 = 0.33$ **(1)**;

   P(GG or SS) $= 0.2 + 0.33 = 0.53$ **(1)**

   (ii) P (different) $= 1 - $ (b)(i) $= 0.47$ **(1)**

2. N(100, 5.9²).

   (a) $P(X > 115) = P\left(z > \dfrac{110 - 100}{5.9}\right)$ **(1)** $\Rightarrow P(z > 1.6949)$ **(1)**,

   $P = 0.04551$ **(1)**

   (b) $P(X > 92) = P\left(z > \dfrac{92 - 100}{5.9}\right)$ **(1)** $\Rightarrow P(z > -1.3559)$,

   $P = 0.08756$ **(1)**

   (c) P(95 < X < 105), P = 0.6032599 (from calculator) ≈ 0.603 **(1)**

3. (a) A Beijing, B Leeming, C Jacksonville

   (2, 1 for two correct answers)

   (b) (i) Between 10 and 12, p = 0.358 **(1)** 11.099 ≈ 11 days **(1)**

   (ii) At least one standard deviation below the mean,

   p = 0.1587 **(1)** 4.9197 days **(1)**

4. (a) H_0: $\mu = 1320$; H_1: $\mu < 1320$ **(1)**; Under H_0,

   $\bar{X} \sim N\left(1320, \dfrac{26.4^2}{6}\right)$, $\sum x = 7780$, $\bar{x} = 1296.6$.

   $\dfrac{1296.7 - 1320}{\sqrt{\dfrac{26.4^2}{6}}} = -2.16186\ldots$ **(1)**

   At 1% significance, $\phi z = 0.01$, $z = -2.32.63$ **(1)**. The observed
   value is in the acceptance region. There is evidence at the 1%
   significance level that the manufacturer's batteries do last as
   long as they claim. ∴ accept H_0 and reject H_1. **(2)**

   (b) $\dfrac{\bar{x} - 1320}{\sqrt{\dfrac{26.4^2}{6}}}$ **(1)** $= -2.3263$; $\bar{x} = 1294.9$ **(1)**

5. (a) Allocate a unique number to each member of the
   population, starting from 0001 **(1)**; use a random number
   generator to generate 30 different numbers and select
   these members of the population for the sample. **(1)**

(b) sample is size 30, so mean is $\dfrac{63800}{30} = 2126.67$ **(1)**

   square root of variance = 913.098 **(1)**

(c) *According to the information provided in the LDS,
   visibility is defined as the greatest distance at which an
   object can be seen and recognized in daylight, or at night
   could be seen and recognized if the general illumination
   were raised to daylight level. Visibility is measured in
   decametres (10m). In the context of this sample, the
   mean visibility for 1987 at Heathrow was 2126.67 Dm
   (21266.7 m, or approximately 21 km) and the standard
   deviation was 913.098 Dm (9130.98 m, or approximately
   9 km)* **(1)**.

6. (a) (i) $X \sim B(15, 0.15)$ **(1)** $P(T_{15} \leq 7) = 0.6535$ (accept 0.654) **(1)**

   (ii) $X \sim B(30, 0.45)$ **(1)**;

   $P(T_{30} \leq 17) - P(T_{30} \leq 12)$ **(1)** $= 0.9286 - 0.3592$
   $= 0.5694$ (accept 0.569) **(1)**

   (b) (i) $n = 5$, $p = 0.45$, $\mu = np = 2.25$ **(1)**;

   variance $= \sigma^2 = np(1 - p) = 2.25(1 - 0.45) = 1.2375$ **(1)**,
   $\sigma = 1.002429773$ (accept 1.11) **(1)**

   (ii) $\sum x = 21$, **(1)** $\bar{x} = 2.1$, **(1)** $\sigma x = 1.13578$ **(1)**
   (accept $sx = 1.1972$)

   (iii) The means are the same, standard deviations are
   slightly different/similar **(1)**.
   Micheal's claim appears valid. **(1)**

EDEXCEL SET 2 PAPER 3 – SECTION B – MECHANICS

7. Resolving vertically, $R = 9g$; using $F \leq \mu R$, $F \leq 0.3 \times 9g$ **(1)**;
   $F \leq 26.46\,\text{N}$ **(1)**

8. (a) $v = \dfrac{ds}{dt} = 2.8t - 0.3t^2$ **(1)**;

   when $t = 6$, $v = 2.8 \times 6 - 0.3 \times 6^2 = 6\,\text{m s}^{-1}$ **(1)**

   (b) $a = \dfrac{d^2 s}{dt^2} = 2.8 - 0.6t$ **(1)**;

   when $t = 6$, $a = 2.8 - 0.6 \times 6 = -0.8\,\text{m s}^{-2}$ **(1)**

   (c) when $t = 0$, $s = 0.4\,\text{m}$ **(1)**

   (d) when $t = 6$, $s = 0.4 + 1.4 \times 6^2 - 0.1 \times 6^3 = 29.2\,\text{m}$ **(1)**;

   average velocity $= \dfrac{\text{final displacement} - \text{initial displacement}}{\text{time}}$

   $= \dfrac{29.2 - 0.4}{6} = 4.8\,\text{m s}^{-1}$ **(1)**

9. (a) Correct diagram **(1 for horizontal forces, 1 for vertical forces)**

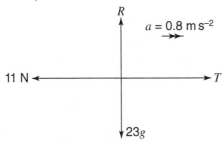

   (b) Using $F = ma$, $T - 11 = ma$ **(1)**;
   $T = ma + 11$, $T = 23 \times 0.8 + 11$ **(1)** $= 29.4\,\text{N}$ **(1)**

10. (a) Diagram **(1 for correct shape, 1 for labels on time axis, 1 for labels on velocity axis)**

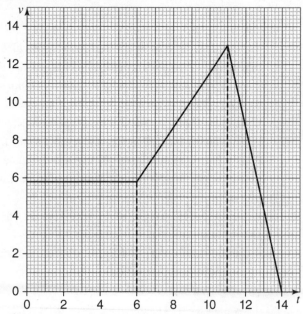

(b) Acceleration $= -\dfrac{13}{3} = -4.333...$ m s^{-2}

(–ve hence deceleration) **(1)**

(c) $5.8 \times 6 = 34.8$; $\dfrac{1}{2}(5.8 + 13) \times 5 = 47$ **(1)**; $\dfrac{1}{2} \times 3 \times 13 = 19.5$ **(1)**;

$34.8 + 47 + 19.5 = 101.3$ m **(1)**

11. (a) $v = (3 + 5t)\mathbf{i} - 11t\mathbf{j}$ **(2)**

(b) $v = (3 + 5 \times 1.5)\mathbf{i} - 11 \times 1.5\mathbf{j} \Rightarrow v = 10.5\mathbf{i} - 16.5\mathbf{j}$ **(1)**;

speed $= \sqrt{10.5^2 + 16.5^2}$ **(1)** $= 19.56$ m s^{-1} **(1)**

12. (a) (1 for fully correct diagram)

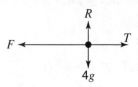

(b) Resolving vertically for 5 kg, $F = ma$, $5g - T = 5a$,

① $T = 5g - 5a$; Resolving vertically for 4 kg, $R = 4g$ **(1)**;

Using $F_{max} = \mu R$, $F_{max} = 0.3 \times 4g = 11.76$ N **(1)**; Resolving

horizontally for 4 kg,

② $T - 11.76 = 4a$ **(1)**. Sub ① into ②: $5g - 5a - 11.76 = 4a$ **(1)**;

$9a = 5g - 11.76$; $9a = 37.24$;

$a = 4.14$ m s^{-2} **(1)**

(c) $T = 5g - 5 \times 4.14$ **(1)** $= 28.3$ N **(1)**

(d) If in equilibrium, resolving vertically for 5 kg,

$T - 5g = 0$, $T = 5g$ **(1)**. If 5 kg is on point of moving

upwards, the 4 kg will be on the point of moving left,

so frictional force F will have the same magnitude as in

(b) but moving in the opposite direction.

$F_{net} = ma$; $P - F - T = 11.76 + 5g$ **(1)**; $P = 60.76$ N **(1)**

13. (a) Diagram **(1 for vertical forces, 1 for correct distances)**

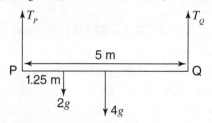

(b) Taking moments about P **(1)**,

$2g \times 1.25 + 4g \times 2.5 = T_Q \times 5$ **(1)**;

$122.5 = 5T_Q$, $T_Q = 24.5$ N **(1)**;

$T_P + T_Q = 6g$ **(1)**; $T_P = 6g - T_Q$; $T_P = 34.3$ N **(1)**

14. (a) Resolving vertically, taking $\uparrow$ as positive, $u = 40\sin 45°$,

$a = -9.8$ m s^{-2}, $s = -2$ m, $t = t$; $s = ut + \dfrac{1}{2}at^2$;

$-2 = 40\sin 45°t + \dfrac{1}{2}(-9.8)t^2$ **(1)** $\Rightarrow 4.9t^2 - 40\sin 45°t - 2 = 0$ **(1)**;

when $x = -0.06$, $t = 5.84$ s **(1)**.

Resolving horizontally, $u = 40\cos 45°$, $a = 0$, $s = s$,

$t = 5.84$ s; $s = 40\cos 45° \times 5.84$ **(1)** $= 165.18$ m **(1)**

(b) Resolving vertically, with $s = 0$,

$0 = 40\sin 45°t + \dfrac{1}{2}(-9.8)t^2$ **(1)**

$\therefore t = 0$ or $t = 5.77$ seconds.

$5.84 - 5.77 = 0.07$ seconds **(1)**

SECTION B : MECHANICS

8. A particle has acceleration $5\,\mathrm{m\,s^{-2}}$ when a force of magnitude 8 N acts upon it.

Find the mass of the particle.

....

....

....

....

(Total 1 mark)

9. A light 6 m long beam hangs from a light, inextensible string.

Two weights are placed on the beam as illustrated in the diagram, so that it is in equilibrium.

(a) Find the tension T in the string. **(1)**

....

....

....

(b) Find the distance s **(2)**

....

....

....

(Total 3 marks)